READING, PRAYING, LIVING
THE US BISHOPS' PASTORAL LETTER
AGAINST RACISM
OPEN WIDE OUR HEARTS

Reading, Praying, Living The US Bishops' Pastoral Letter Against Racism Open Wide Our Hearts

A Faith Formation Guide

Alison M. Benders

LITURGICAL PRESS
Collegeville, Minnesota

www.litpress.org

1   2   3   4   5   6   7   8   9

Library of Congress Cataloging-in-Publication Data

Names: Benders, Alison M., author.
Title: Reading, praying, living the US bishops' pastoral letter against racism, Open wide our hearts : a faith formation guide / Alison M. Benders.
Description: Collegeville, Minnesota : Liturgical Press, 2020. | Includes bibliographical references. | Summary: "A resource designed to help parishes, RCIA programs, campus ministries, and Catholic readers unpack and grapple with the U.S. bishops' new document on racism"— Provided by publisher.
Identifiers: LCCN 2019034930 (print) | LCCN 2019034931 (ebook) | ISBN 9780814665015 (paperback) | ISBN 9780814665268 (pdf) | ISBN 9780814665268 (epub) | ISBN 9780814665268 (mobi)
Subjects: LCSH: Catholic Church. United States Conference of Catholic Bishops. Open wide our hearts. | Racism—Religious aspects—Catholic Church. | Catholic Church—Doctrines. | Catholic Church—United States.
Classification: LCC BX1795.R33 B46 2020 (print) | LCC BX1795.R33 (ebook) | DDC 282/.73089—dc23
LC record available at https://lccn.loc.gov/2019034930
LC ebook record available at https://lccn.loc.gov/2019034931

For my husband, Larry, and our children

Contents

Acknowledgments

I could not have written this guide without the support and encouragement of a wide community of generous people. This community includes my colleagues and the students at the Jesuit School of Theology who have challenged my presumptions and shared their experiences; the amazing parish family at St. Columba Church whose warmth and acceptance are teaching me how to live more justly; and my own family and friends who have joined me in a decades-long quest to understand racism and white privilege in US culture, past and present. My debt to others is immeasurable. I offer my deepest gratitude to those I mention here and so many others for their patience with me.

Introduction

"If we wish to serve God and love our neighbor well, we must manifest our joy in the service we render to Him and to them. Let us open wide our hearts" (16).[1] So insisted St. Katharine Drexel, the first saint born in the United States. Mother Drexel founded the Sisters of the Blessed Sacrament and committed herself to serving Native American and African American communities during her long life, spanning the end of slavery to the beginning of the Civil Rights movement. The United States Conference of Catholic Bishops' recent pastoral letter against racism invites her protection by its title, Open Wide Our Hearts. The letter's essential theme is love. It describes a humble and expansive love that respects human dignity and unites us all into a community in Christ. The bishops teach us that racism denies full human dignity to some people in our society.

We see racism at work in the superiority that some people feel over others and, even more so, in the structures and habits of our communities that privilege some and disinherit others. Racism has inflicted untold violence, strife, oppression, and alienation in our nation for centuries. "Racism directly places brother and sister against each other, violating the dignity inherent in each person," the bishops write (25). They call us to

> The end of racism will not come through prayer and hope alone.

model our lives on Christ's love, which unites all people into one human family. The letter is a renewed, deeper, and more urgent call to conversion. The bishops invite us to eradicate racism in all its forms through hearts that are wide open in active love. We can respond with converted minds to understand what racism is, with converted hearts to recognize its destructiveness for individuals and society, and with converted actions that purposefully aim to create a just community in our nation and our church.

The United States Conference of Catholic Bishops published Open Wide Our Hearts in late 2018.[2] Released nearly forty years after their prior pastoral statement on racism,[3] this letter seeks to reignite our passion for racial justice in order to eradicate America's "original sin" (4). The bishops sketch out both past and present sins. They recognize that the church's response to racism largely has been silence, a silence that is inconsistent with the principles of Catholic social thought and with our faith. The bishops ask for forgiveness for their own racial sins and pledge themselves to the struggle to heal the racial divide. Most importantly, they have opened the door for the rest of us to reflect seriously on racism and to commit ourselves to building a more just community. As Catholics, we profess to believe that Christ's love unites all people into one body. This letter calls us to both conversion and action to root out racism. The bishops close with this most urgent message: "We pray that the reader will join us in striving for the end of racism in all its forms, that we may walk together humbly with God and with all of our brothers and sisters in a renewed unity" (26).

The end of racism will not come through prayer and hope alone. A conversion of our national culture, as the letter instructs us, will occur only through our intentional efforts to reform the cultural, political, legal, and structural impediments to every person's full participation in society. We must be seriously committed to a shared future, in which the color of people's skin

or their family ancestry truly does not matter. The unacknowl-
edged difficulty is the real and painful challenge of reconciling
people after centuries of such profound divisions and violence.
The legacy of slavery, Jim Crow laws, and segregation continue
in our legal system and practices. They perpetuate past legacies of
oppression and exclusion. Healing our racial wounds, for some,
will mean reliving personal traumas, threats to life and safety, and
daily injustices. For others, it will mean guilt, embarrassment,
indignation, and coping with unearned advantages.

For all of us, healing racial injustice must mean
humbly embracing our common history, the times
when we have repeatedly valued one group over
another simply because of inherited differences
and imposed social stigmas. Our nation has focused harmfully on difference rather than on the
unity of humanity that reflects God's infinite love
in the varieties of our gifts and perspectives. While
we must certainly speak of cultural and systemic racism, racial
justice is always a call to personal conversion that yields social
and structural transformation. Racial justice requires us to reflect
on how we have suffered as a fragmented and divided nation and
how we, as a united people, can forge a culture for our nation
that is no longer premised on exploitation and marginalization.
If racism can be uprooted, our tools must be the Spirit's gifts of
humility, love, and courage.

> Racial justice is always a call to personal conversion.

This study guide, then, aims to help parishes and faith groups
unpack Open Wide Our Hearts. We will start with an overview
of Catholic social thought and the prominent themes in the
social encyclicals of the church. After that, we will learn why the
bishops' letter is so timely and how it came to be published after
a careful process of study and writing. Finally, we will highlight
several themes to guide our study of Open Wide Our Hearts,
section by section, in the later chapters of this guide.

What Is Catholic Social Teaching?

Open Wide Our Hearts, directed to Catholics in the United States, expresses the church's teachings on how we can together build a more racially just society. The letter is modeled on the style of papal encyclicals, which are official Roman Catholic church teachings that popes address to all Catholics and often to all people of good will throughout the world. Generally, encyclicals instruct readers on Catholic perspectives about social issues or on matters of doctrine or liturgical practice. Popes sign encyclicals in their own names to show that the letters are their own instructions to the clergy and laity of the church.

The social encyclicals, collectively known as Catholic social teaching or Catholic social thought, are the church's major writings about our lives together in society. Their topics include labor, family and marriage, economic justice, and the life of faith.[4] Pope Francis has authored two encyclicals: Praise Be to You—On Care For Our Common Home (*Laudato Si*, May 24, 2015), which addresses the global ecological crisis; and The Light of Faith (*Lumen Fidei*, June 29, 2013), which explains the Catholic faith in the current global culture and reiterates our principal beliefs. Pope Francis's writings have been praised for their pastoral tone. He uses metaphors to convey vividly how we are to think about our Christian lives. Famously, he painted the church in the image of a "field hospital" located in the heart of our suffering world, working to heal people's lives and relationships. The pope's major themes have been mercy and the integral or intertwined nature of all life and all human communities.

We can find inspiration to live with each other in more just and loving ways.

Although encyclicals are anchored in pressing social or economic concerns, the letters put specific issues into the broader context of a flourishing human community in which our lives enflesh God's love for all people. Encyclicals explore issues through a combination of scriptural background, theological interpretation, and moral formation. They may offer deep historical-critical analysis by relying on expert studies of the issues as the foundation for the formation in the letters. The teachings customarily offer a specific scriptural and theological lens so that readers can understand how to reflect on their concerns and how to form their consciences to live the Gospel more fully.

The social encyclicals are not catechism, because their purpose is not to define what Catholics must believe. They do not suggest public policies to be enacted as laws. Rather, social encyclicals, such as the widely acclaimed *Laudato Si*, aim for moral-religious-personal transformation rather than programs and remedies. Social encyclicals connect society's current issues with Scripture's stories and parables to inspire our imaginative reflection. They invite us to live our love for God more intentionally within our local communities and in relationship with all people. Through a new vision of what ought to be, especially lessons from Jesus' life and ministry, we find inspiration to live with each other in more just and loving ways.[5] Open Wide Our Hearts sits squarely within this social encyclical tradition.

What Is Open Wide Our Hearts About?

Although racism is a global social issue, Open Wide Our Hearts is a pastoral letter from the bishops of the United States to instruct Catholics about racism in our country. The bishops seek to guide us to conversion—to change our hearts—followed by deliberate actions to create more just communities in our nation. As Catholic readers, we appreciate the gravity and urgency of racism because the bishops of the United States, as a whole, affirmed this letter. Open Wide Our Hearts addresses every Catholic in every diocese in our nation. We must take the bishops' words to heart and respond.

The long-standing evil of racism, as well as current "episodes of violence and animosity with racial and xenophobic overtones" occurring in our communities, motivated the bishops to write this pastoral letter.[6] In August 2017, the president of the US Conference of Catholic Bishops started the process by appointing the Ad Hoc Committee Against Racism, now led by Bishop Shelton J. Fabre of the Houma-Thibodaux diocese in Louisiana. The USCCB charged the ad hoc committee to unite Catholics together as a church and as members of society to find ways to heal racism through the pastoral guidance they can offer. Aiming for a tone of pastoral care, they wanted a letter that inspired reflection, contrition, and conversion. They recognized that when people change their hearts, the new commitment "then multiplies, [and] will compel change and reform in our institutions and society."[7] The letter continues the teaching in Brothers and Sisters to Us: A Pastoral Letter on Racism from 1979. However, as culture and social conditions in the United States have changed in four decades, Open Wide Our Hearts offers a more nuanced and more insistent call for a love that will nurture a community of healing and justice.

To inspire a vision of such a community in Christ, the new letter incorporates both Scripture and the principles of Catholic social teaching going back more than one hundred years. The letter provides a structure for understanding racism as a sin and calls us to convert our hearts and minds. Many of the themes are familiar to us:

- All human beings are created in the image of God.

- Jesus proclaimed and inaugurated God's reign of justice.

- We are one community united in Christ—the Body of Christ—and governed by love, justice, and human dignity.

- Care for the poor and marginalized is a special mark of the Christian community.

Building on these principles, Open Wide Our Hearts emphasizes that racism is a profound failure to love—a failure to recognize the image of God in each and every person. We read again and again in this letter the theme of conversion, which is essential for a more just community.

More specifically, Open Wide Our Hearts builds upon the bishops' letter of 1979, Brothers and Sisters to Us. This second letter updates events in the forty-year interval and reflects the US church's deepening awareness of the complexity of racial privilege and oppression. For one thing, the letter identifies racism as more than bigotry and intolerance. Through the course of the letter, the bishops touch on five important topics:

1. historical violence specifically mentioning Native Americans, African Americans, and those of Hispanic descent;

2. implicit bias and racial attitudes that influence actions, even when we don't realize it;

3. legacies of past wounds, such as the legal and social structures that perpetuate oppression and marginalization;

4. cultural values and norms that rank individuals according to skin color and heritage; and

5. the church's own complicity in what it has done and failed to do about racial justice over centuries in the Americas.

The letter tries to offer a balanced perspective by highlighting saints and heroes from various racial backgrounds who have struggled for racial justice. Significantly, the bishops apologize for their individual and collective racist actions and ask for forgiveness. This contrition models conversion of heart for those of us who read the letter. In fact, the bishops' mood of contrition weaves together the main themes and draws us into the urgent call to heal the racial injustice that wounds our nation. Open Wide Our Hearts ends on a practical but urgent note to every Catholic believer and to all Catholic offices and organizations: We are called to open wide our hearts so that "we will not cease to speak forcefully against and work toward ending racism" (25). The responsibility rests with each of us to create a community of love that will usher in God's reign of justice. The letter closes with a prayer to Mary, the Mother of God.

Many Catholics have welcomed the letter against racism. Some think it has been too long delayed and says too little. More than a few Catholics have puzzled over why this topic is urgent when environmental degradation threatens all life on the planet and the clergy sexual abuse revelations undermine the very unity of our church. Still others are frustrated and dismayed with the letter because it seems to sidestep fundamental questions of white identity, white privilege, and white supremacy.

> There is an urgent call to heal the racial injustice that wounds our nation.

There are several things to understand about the timing of the letter and how the USCCB came to approve it. First, no social teaching stands alone. No issue affecting our human dignity and shared life can be separated from our fundamental commitment to love God and others. Rather, all issues for our human society are linked. Pope Francis in *Laudato Si* preaches about an "integral ecology," showing us how all creation is connected and all our actions are intertwined to destroy or heal the earth. Our commitment to a clean planet and environmental health for all species will support our grandchildren's flourishing in the decades ahead. Likewise, when we live from hearts committed to dignity and respect for all human beings, we consequently become more aware of the way we treat our environment, organize our communities, and spend our money. When we treat others as our brothers and sisters because we are all created in the image of God, we become sensitive to their suffering. Their suffering becomes our concern. So this letter stands within more sustained efforts by the church in the United States, especially by individual bishops, to promote racial and ethnic dignity and to eradicate racism with all its effects.[8]

The letter also responds to a special urgency in our nation due to escalating divisions between political positions and cultural groups. We know that people of color disproportionately suffer injury and death at the hands of law enforcement. Open Wide Our Hearts names a few of the victims, although the bishops recognize that many people who have lost their lives or freedom because of racial injustices go unnamed. No day goes by without media reports about racial privilege, battles over historical legacies and celebrations, unequal impact of laws and legal enforcement, or the biased impact of social and economic policies. While there has been some progress toward a more just society in the United States, we have seen rising racial tensions in the past decade because white privilege seems so intractable. The so-called great recession of 2008 fanned the flames of conflict and exacerbated poverty, especially among many non-white people. The frustration of those excluded and disinherited due to race remains a perpetual and shameful reminder that racial justice has been long, long delayed. Open Wide Our Hearts recognizes that "racism still infects" our national culture (1).

> The church at all levels must work for racial justice.

In their pastoral capacity, the bishops reiterate the basic Christian witness that all people are formed in the image and likeness of God. They call us, as people of faith, to turn from our sins. Using the words of the prophet Micah, they write:

> You have been told, O mortal, what is good,
>   and what the LORD requires of you:
> Only to do justice and to love goodness,
>   and to walk humbly with your God. (Mic 6:8)

These watchwords shape the letter, which ends with specific directions about how the church at all levels must work for racial justice.

How Can This Study Guide Help Us?

The US bishops have explicitly asked all Catholics to fight to eradicate racism. Given the letter's brevity (a mere 61 paragraphs long), Catholics who want to live up to the call of Open Wide Our Hearts will need assistance. Finding ourselves in the national "story of race" requires soul-searching and honesty, regardless of our identity.[9] This study guide will lead us through the letter, section by section. As a first step, we'll investigate the context for the letter and learn more about racism, privilege, and culture, drawing a bit on sociology. The later three sections of the letter track the prophet Micah's words according to themes of justice, goodness, and humility, as will this guide:

1. *Do Justice*—explaining our tragic and sinful history of racism to convert our minds;

2. *Love Goodness*—providing scriptural, theological, and moral guidance to form our consciences to convert our hearts; and

3. *Walk Humbly with God*—setting forth how we can convert our actions.

Because the work of racial healing is a journey, not an event, each chapter of the guide also includes questions for reflection and study, and a prayer that meets the feelings and demands of the chapter. An appendix at the back of the book offers resources organized by topic to support our continuing conversion toward racial justice, eliminating racial privilege, and healing our culture.

Understanding racial reconciliation and working toward healing ourselves is a community project. This difficult topic challenges us to listen to things that may be hard to hear, examine our attitudes and actions honestly, and live in new ways that we might never have foreseen. Talking and writing about race, for me, has been a journey of tremendous growth accompanied by stark revelations of my own blind spots and by moments of humiliation. My own background as a white woman, married and raising children with a man of color, privileged with the opportunity of an academic career at a Jesuit university—all of this has allowed me to live what I study and to study what I am living about racial injustice and racial healing. Nevertheless, I recognize that my own biases and presumptions will appear in this guide. I draw on examples and lessons from my own experiences. For the narrowness and biases in this guide, I ask the readers for indulgence and forgiveness. I trust that we share the hope for a better future for the generations to come.

We are called to open wide our hearts so that together we may forge a more loving and more just community. We are strengthened by God's grace to sustain us as we yearn for a community where we truly live as sisters and brothers in Christ. In the synagogue in Nazareth, as Jesus started his public ministry, he read from the prophet Isaiah:

"The Spirit of the Lord is upon me,
　　because he has anointed me
　　　　to bring glad tidings to the poor.
He has sent me to proclaim liberty to captives
　　and recovery of sight to the blind,
　　　　to let the oppressed go free,
and to proclaim a year acceptable to the Lord. . . ."
He said to them, "Today this scripture passage is fulfilled in
your hearing." (Luke 4:18-19, 21)

Today is the time for our conversion. We start where we are
now—in parish communities, in schools, at our workplaces, and
with our families and friends. We must live out Jesus' liberat-
ing love in our own nation—striving with converted hearts to
eradicate racism and build just communities. Let's begin the
work of racial healing.

1 Getting Our Bearings on Culture, Racial Privilege, and Conversion

Writing about racial injustice is an enormous challenge by any measure. We often do not know what language to use or whether to start with our nation's past sins or with our present injustices. Racism seems so evidently wrong, yet it remains a "particularly . . . persistent form of evil . . . [It] still infects our nation" after four centuries (1). As Catholics in the United States, we need to acknowledge racial injustice as the sin that distorts our communities, large and small. But confronting racism can often be painful, shameful, and even explosive. Through Open Wide Our Hearts, the US bishops urge us to examine our consciences on this sin with the goal of repentance and permanent change to eradicate racism. Love and justice provide the lens for renewal, but to love justly requires a profound, deliberate reorientation of our hearts, minds, and actions.

So let's get our bearings on what we are talking about. This chapter will focus on the letter's introductory section answering the question: "What Is Racism?" Here, the letter describes what racism is and gives examples, which the bishops revisit with more detail in later sections. The introduction closes with a call for conversion, in the words of the prophet Micah: Do justice, love goodness, and walk humbly with God.

What Is Racism?

The subtitle of the letter, The Enduring Call to Love, stakes out its key theme. God calls us to love and invites us into union in Christ. Racism in our personal relationships and in our institutions is evil because it destroys the unity of the human community. This first section sets forth the problem, describes racism and then explains that it is a sin against justice. Our faith tells us that all people are children of God so that everyone is entitled to respect, dignity, and a just distribution of God's gracious gifts. We are one human family united in Christ. The letter references the Gospel of Matthew to remind us of the second great commandment: "You shall love your neighbor as yourself" (Matt 22:39). This means that our love must include all people and assure for everyone the full benefits of a just community.

Racism contradicts Christ's fundamental commandment to love one another, the bishops teach us. Our failure to love fully divides our human communities, particularly in this country. Racism "judges persons of other races or ethnicities as inferior and unworthy of equal regard" (1). The letter teaches that racism arises when a person holds the false belief that another person or group is inferior due to race or ethnicity and this leads to injustice, evidenced by discrimination, mistreatment, and exclusion. This emphasizes that racism is a personal attitude plus an action. Racism is a "destructive and persistent" evil "because a person ignores the fundamental truth that, because all humans share a common origin, they are all brothers and sisters, all equally made in the image of God. When this truth is ignored, the consequence is prejudice and fear of the other, and—all too often—hatred" (1–2). Theologian Margaret Guider offers this complementary definition of racism, encapsulating the bishops'

> Racism destroys the unity of the human community.

teaching. She writes that racism is "a system by which one race maintains supremacy over another race through a set of attitudes, behaviors, social structures, ideologies, and the requisite power needed to impose them."[1] The power of racism as a sin derives from the dominant group's power to exclude others from the good things in life.

Racism is sometimes called America's "original sin" because it stretches back to the sixteenth century with the arrival of Europeans in the Western Hemisphere (4). Europeans exploring and colonizing the American continents justified the genocide of the indigenous peoples and the enslavement of Africans. The Europeans failed to recognize the people of different cultures and identities as human beings worthy of respect, dignity, and love. These attitudes and actions are the root of an ongoing pattern of racial injustice that marks our original and enduring sin in this nation.

The letter then articulates the varieties of racism that persist today. The bishops remind us of the suffering and violence that men and women of color encounter daily, directing our full attention to the viciousness and volatility of racism. In listing specific examples, the pastoral letter points out the ethnic, racial, and religious harassment reported every day in the news media. Expressing superiority through comments and disparaging jokes injures others, just as much as violent symbols "such as nooses and swastikas" do (2). The bishops note that people's silence—our own silence—in the face of racial injustice is itself a sin, a "*sin of omission*" (2, emphasis added). Both personal actions and systemic exclusions are racial injuries that result when we do not consider others worthy of our regard, when we refuse to acknowledge the full human dignity of people of color.

> The power of racism as a sin derives from the dominant group's power to exclude others from the good things in life.

The letter particularly highlights racially unjust structures. Interlocking laws, policies, and customs create systemic and institutional acts of racism, perpetuating rather than repairing past racist oppressions. Unjust systems include injustices stemming from housing segregation, employment discrimination, and disparate educational funding (2). The inequitable enforcement of criminal laws against non-whites is another vivid example, whether it occurs in policing, in courtroom outcomes, or in the prison system (2–3). We often hear about over-policing, which refers to greater police suspicion of communities of color and enforcing criminal laws vigorously against them for less serious infractions. Whether consciously or not, our cultural attitudes pronounce that people of color, compared to whites, are less valuable, less industrious, or more likely to break the law. The bishops admit that regardless of our individual goodwill the "cumulative effects of personal sins of racism have led to social structures of injustice and violence that make us all accomplices" (3).

We need to pause here in reading the letter to address two very sensitive and important aspects of racism. It will help to understand more about structural racism as embedded in the culture, institutions, and laws in our nation and about how racial privilege works.

Understanding Structural Racism

Structural racism highlights an important distinction between the personal sins of racism and the social structures of injustice, sometimes called a "culture" of racism. Personal sins include racist actions, such as refusing to socialize with someone of a different background or using racially charged slurs (as the bishops mention). These are painful to people and can be quite violent and harmful. But intolerant actions alone are not enough to sustain a racially unjust culture. We can still have "racism without racists."[2] We actually need a more nuanced understanding of culture and social group power.

The term culture stands for our community's way of interacting that is anchored in our shared values and meanings, including our stories about how we came to be and what we hope for in the future.[3] The sociology of culture studies how people articulate what is important to them as they live together or share a project. Communities develop symbols, values, beliefs, norms, and language to express and preserve their lives together. The cultural expressions are clear to a community's members but can be obscure to outsiders who do not understand the references or the shared history. After a while, the laws of a community take on a life of their own, becoming almost unbreakable, because people forget why they originally made these choices and policies.

To help us understand how culture works, let's explore the following diagram and then examine one example from our US culture, the "American Dream." In the diagram below, the pyramid locates culture as central to community, values, and daily life. Essential community values develop from years of living together, organizing the members' ways of life, and allowing them to solve common problems. Over time, a community's values become embedded in their expressions and interactions. Often local laws and public policies will presume and preserve the communities' sensibilities, even without anyone expressly demanding this. Therefore, past values and customs continue for years and generations in the community's culture, apart from any one person deliberately deciding to keep the past alive.

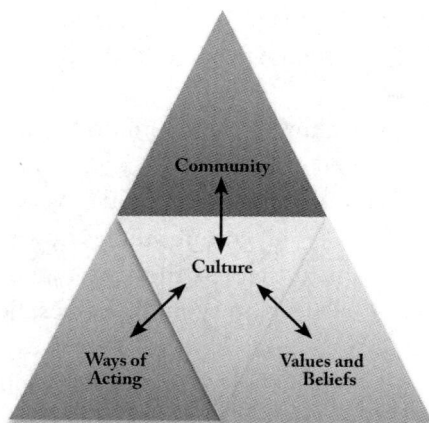

Let's consider an example of how culture works. Our nation values education. Public schools assure that every child will be able to participate in our democracy and will be prepared for employment. When the practice of tax-funded public schools emerged in the nineteenth century, there was no school in the summer because children needed to help out on the family farm. Now in the twenty-first century, most towns still do not require summer classes even though only a small percentage of US families farm for a living. Our past economic choices have created the culture that constrains us today.

So, we can notice how we take for granted that the school year must run from fall through spring or early summer. The school year is now nine months because we used to need children on the family farm. Notice also how many of our other institutions are built upon the school year/summer break foundation, including back-to-school sales in August, summer hours for offices, and daylight saving time. The nine-month school year has become natural, obvious, and even required. Thus, the initial convention has become locked-in and reinforced by other practices over nearly two centuries.

Open Wide Our Hearts refers to the idea of locked-in conventions where it reads, "Racism can often be found in our hearts—in many cases placed there unwillingly or unknowingly by our upbringing and culture" (2). Sociologist Eduardo Bonilla-Silva explains that racism persists when people use a racial framework to explain and communicate how the world works, even without realizing it.[4] Our national framework includes using race to explain personal differences, assign burdens, categorize abilities, and differentiate groups. A cultural framework can become self-legitimizing, meaning that we do not have to explain or justify it; it just is what we have always done. Racial frameworks are especially problematic because they are so vague. They depend on the interpretation of complex circumstances, which allows contradictions and exceptions within the overarching structure. This makes people oblivious to the basic irrationality of dividing and judging people based on physical traits, such as skin color.

When we think about it, we recognize that presumptions about racial superiority are deeply embedded in our cultural structures because of past attitudes. These presumptions, like many cultural legacies, profoundly constrain us because that is how culture works. When we examine these cultural values, we can see that they are historical choices made by our ancestors. Sometimes the choices were based on important priorities, such as free speech and religious freedom. Sometimes the choices were good when they were made, but they no longer apply because our circumstances have changed, like the nine-month school year. Sometimes the choices were evil, like laws that enslaved or excluded others based on racial identity, because the people who came before us had a deeply flawed appreciation of human physical and cultural diversity.

A much more complex and challenging example of how our culture defines us is the idea of the American Dream. We examine it here because it is closely tied to racial identity, even

> The American Dream is elusive for many people because of locked-in racism.

though we often miss the connection. The American Dream encapsulates our proud history of working from "rags to riches." We believe that everyone can succeed with hard work and persistence. People of other nations dream of immigrating to our country because they share the hope of making a better life for their children. The American Dream in the nineteenth century included "a chicken in every pot" or, in the twentieth century, living in a stable neighborhood with a house, a yard, and a school nearby for the kids. The specifics differ in the twenty-first century from prior eras, but the American Dream continues to live in our imaginations and define one of our fundamental values.

While "America" can mean opportunity, hard work, and making a meaningful life for ourselves and those we love, it often is not a real possibility for many groups in our nation. The actual opportunity for a good life is profoundly entwined with racial categories and racial oppression. It is elusive for many people, no matter how hard they work because of locked-in racism. Consider this example. In our country success often is measured in terms of income (earnings per year) and wealth (the value of what a family owns). However, statistical evidence shows that income and wealth are not equal across racial groups. Since the mid-1980s, the net wealth of white households has increased, while the net wealth of non-white households has decreased substantially.[5] A 2017 Pew Research report, *How Wealth Inequality Has Changed in the U.S. since the Great Recession*, provides these data-based conclusions for the past ten years:

- Among lower- and middle-income households, white families have four times as much wealth as black families and three times as much as Hispanic families.

- Wealth gaps between upper-income families and lower- and middle-income families [in 2017] are at the highest levels recorded [for our nation].
- Upper-income white families have grown wealthier [since 2008, while other groups have not].[6]

Similar data can be found to show the racial disparities in salaries, educational achievement, professional success, health outcomes and lifespan, and incarceration rates.[7]

These statistics, as well as our own experiences, challenge us to consider why racial differences in wealth exist and are becoming even worse, especially if we assert that the American Dream is a real possibility for everyone. Why do these disparities exist if all of us are beloved by God, God is gracious to all, and we are all brothers and sisters in Christ? We realize that our individual situations—where we were born, who our parents are, our race or ethnicity, how much money our family has, how good our schools were—will open or close doors for us.[8] Despite hard work and an intense desire to do well, most people born into families without education and jobs will remain on the lower end of the economic scale.[9] The American Dream is not a reality for all people equally in this nation. We can ask ourselves if we believe that differences are "natural" among different groups or whether some people suffer impediments that others do not, and what these might be.

More to the point, we must appreciate that many of our apparently neutral cultural symbols actually carry embedded presumptions about racial identity and value. Even the categories of race or racial identity are cultural conventions. Our next section, therefore, will explore what we mean by race as a cultural category. We will also consider the privileges that racial classifications offer and the burdens they impose on groups in our society.

Race and Racial Privilege

To really embrace the call to conversion in Open Wide Our Hearts and eradicate racism, we must not shy away from directly discussing the meaning of race. Because our cultural values are often invisible, as we just discussed, we need to look very hard at racial categories. We often use race or color to identify people, but these labels are quite slippery. When someone claims to be "white" or we say someone is "black," it is much different than saying "my shoe size is 8" or "he's tall." Our labels about skin color, race, and ethnicity actually conceal a whole series of social and cultural judgments about who people are.

We tend to consider race to be a fundamental aspect of human identity. Perhaps we even think of race as natural and inherited and that our categories are determined by obvious physical attributes only. Certainly, our genes determine the shade of our skin, the shape of our features, and the texture of our hair. But genetic scientists confirm that there are no DNA markers or physical tests to divide people neatly into so-called color groups or ethnic communities.

Let's try another thought experiment. Reflect now on the way people featured in the media are labeled white, African American, Hispanic American, or Asian American. Think about the appearance of civic leaders, entertainers, professional athletes, and everyday people we see in videos. Many individuals who share the same racial label have quite varied physical qualities. We can notice how we label people according to features and skin tone as well as according to social, political, and economic categories. The information we use to apply a racial label may include where people live, who their parents are, their income, education and speech patterns, and even their music or clothing preferences. Very often our choice to use a particular label for a person shows what we think is important about them. When we are honest, we must acknowledge that a person's racial label (whether they claim it or we ascribe it to them) means something much more than observable traits. Unfortunately, the way we label people has vital consequences for them in our society.

To understand the consequences of racial labels, we must confront the idea of privilege. We hear the expressions "racial privilege" or "white privilege" in discussions about racism in the media and in daily conversation. Privilege sounds like an accusatory term, but there is a better way to understand what it means. In our society people have all sorts of privileges. Some privileges are earned and well deserved; some are not. Some privileges are just for fun, but many can be oppressive and deadly serious. We can think of a privilege as an advantage, like a teenager who earns the privilege of using the family car through good grades or a traveler who has applied for TSA pre-check for faster security screening at airports. We see television commercials that tout "wealth has its privileges" meaning that people who have money can enjoy life at resorts with fine wine and international cuisine.

Privilege refers generally to a positive or affirmative advantage. When we benefit from an affirmative privilege, others in our circles often share that advantage directly and indirectly. For example, if I own a car, I can drive to work and not be tied to the bus schedule. With a dependable car, I have greater flexibility for work hours and locations. This means I have an advantage in the job market because I have more job choices. Being securely employed (salary, benefits, and preferred location) also means that I have a network of coworkers and friends who likewise are well employed and economically self-sufficient. Perhaps I can leverage my employment advantage into job connections for my children, my siblings, or my friends. In this example, one affirmative privilege translates into a series

> To understand the consequences of racial labels, we must confront the idea of privilege.

of benefits. I am not burdened by the transportation problems that those without a car face, and I can use my situation to help other people I know. An affirmative privilege becomes racial privilege when we extend our own advantages to others of our same ethnicity or race.[10]

A second kind of privilege is restrictive. It refers to withholding advantages from some people. As the opposite of affirmative privilege, restrictive privilege encompasses what we refuse to do for others, how we refuse to give them the "benefit of the doubt." Let's try another thought experiment, this time about someone needing help. Imagine someone comes to your door for help because her car has broken down. If she is your neighbor, you'll help her immediately. If her clothes, grooming, and words are similar to your own or those of your neighbors, you are also likely to help her. The fact that we're talking about a woman may also have something to do with your decision. Now imagine that a man comes to your door asking for the same help with the same words, but he dresses and speaks in ways that are not familiar to you. What goes through your mind in deciding to help or to give the benefit of the doubt to the person at your door?

Restrictive privilege operates in this example. Our neighbors get advantages from being neighbors, and rightly so. But when people who are different from us approach us, we are less likely to give them the benefit of the doubt. We scrutinize them more suspiciously. We can see how we often make judgments based on cultural presumptions rather than observable facts. Whether or not we deny privileges to others is very often related to what race we label them. The presumptions dictate whether we think of another person as "one of us" or whether we can justifiably ignore their problems.[11] The point of this example is not to suggest unwarranted trust but to encourage us to reflect on our cultural presumptions, which are active in even the most mundane exchanges.

As we close this discussion of privilege (and there is so much more to say), we must embrace an important point for construc-

tive conversations around race. Categories of
race and practices of racial privilege are
some of the deepest, most violent divisions in our nation stretching back centuries. For good reason, racism is "our
country's original sin" (4). Even our
brief thought experiments show how
racial categories and privileges are locked
in. Although we have not made an individual
decision to adopt distorted racial values, categories
about race and ethnicity govern our social interactions, often with
heartbreaking consequences.

> We can
> eliminate unjust
> racial privilege when
> we recognize how it
> perpetuates sinful and
> unjust structures at
> every level of our
> shared lives.

In concluding our discussion of structural racism and racial
privilege, here is the main point. Cultural structures and race-
based privileges lock in racism. Even without our personal ill will
or attitudes of superiority, cultural structures will endure unless
we actually reconfigure our lives together to provide full dignity
and opportunity for all people in our nation. To the extent we
know about racial injustice and take no steps to eliminate it, we
can be considered complicit in it. We have reason to hope, however. Because communities of people create cultures, people can
change cultures. We can eliminate unjust racial privilege when
we recognize how it works and, in particular, how it perpetuates
sinful and unjust structures at every level of our shared lives.

We'll come back to reforming culture when we move to the
next section of the letter, *To Do Justice*, in chapter 2. First, we
need to discuss the bishops' final point in this section: conversion.

Conversion

With an overview of the starkest and most disturbing racial
injustices before our eyes, Open Wide Our Hearts calls us to
a "genuine conversion of heart" (4). Genuine conversion must

be personal, as well as a conversion of our church and our communities. Conversion means a radical change of heart that leads to a radical change in behavior, a theme that runs throughout Scripture. The New Testament Greek uses the term *metanoia*, which has sometimes been translated as conversion of mind or heart, and sometimes as repentance. Jesus began his ministry in Galilee calling, "Repent, for the kingdom of heaven is at hand" (Matt 4:17). Conversion means adopting a completely new way of living with others.

Calling us to conversion, Open Wide Our Hearts aims to address both the causes of racism and the harms that flow from it (4–5). Conversion necessarily includes our profound realization—even remorse—when we grasp how far we have strayed from God's call to love. When our conversion is authentic, our new values shape our behavior and we strive to live with integrity to make sure they come alive in our lives. In *Laudato Sì*, Pope Francis defines conversion as "heartfelt repentance and desire to change" (218). Open Wide Our Hearts reminds us: "Moving our nation to a full realization of the promise of liberty, equality, and justice *for all* is even more challenging [than individual conversion and action]" (4, emphasis original). Structures of racism are powerful, often oppressing people despite the fact that they are not intended. Conversion in a community setting must yield a new configuration. Our lives together must be restructured because our hearts are converted and realigned to love each other as God loves us.

The introduction to Open Wide Our Hearts concludes with Micah's powerful judgment:

> You have been told, O mortal, what is good,
>   and what the LORD requires of you:
> Only to do justice and to love goodness,
>   and to walk humbly with your God. (Mic 6:8, cited at 5)

The bishops use this quotation as a road map for conversion and justice. Doing justice means recognizing what justice is and how our national history is a story of injustice for so many people. Loving goodness requires us to examine our national and personal history through the lens of God's love as it is revealed in Scripture. Walking humbly with God demands that our love becomes visible, with the steps that the final section of the letter outlines. We turn now to *Do Justice*.

Questions for Reflection

1. Instead of thinking about racial labels as fixed and objective (like a person's shoe size), what happens when we realize that these categories are judgments about how important a person is?

2. Where have you noticed privilege working for or against you? What would a privilege-free society feel like for you and those you love?

Questions for Study

1. Consider the discussion above about culture and study the diagram. Can you give an example of a cultural value or symbol and use the diagram to trace how it works? Can you identify a symbol that is related to race or ethnic identity?

2. Watch this short video on "Defining the American Dream" (2009) by New York Times journalist Shayla Harris, found online at https://www.nytimes.com/video /us/1194840031120/defining-the-american-dream.html.

   • What is the American Dream in your own words?

- Which groups in our nation have (and have not) achieved the American Dream? Other than personal talents, what else influences or impedes people's likelihood of securing the American Dream?

Prayer for Open Hearts and Conversion

Good and gracious God, you love each of us with a wide-open love. We pray for our own conversion and the conversion of all your faithful people.

Wake us up to justice!

Racial injustice in our nation and in the world surrounds us and infects us. We hear it in the media, see it in our communities, and recognize it in our mistrusting relationships and personal divisions. We bring these experiences and our broken hearts to you now. We are overwhelmed with the profound sin of our nation.

Wake us up to justice!

We ask you for humble spirits and open hearts to journey from the shackles of racial oppression into the joys of a just community. As a eucharistic community united in Jesus' self-giving love, impassion us to embody justice in our lives together. We are embraced and secure in the breadth and depth of your wide-open love.

Wake us up to justice! Amen.

2 Do Justice
Converting Our Minds

Our conversion work continues in earnest with the letter's section titled *Do Justice* (8–17). The discussion helps us grasp why racism is such sinful injustice. First, we will investigate the bishops' explanation of injustice theologically as "lust to dominate" (6, quoting St. Augustine). Then, we will focus on the histories of three groups of people as they are highlighted in Open Wide Our Hearts. After drawing out the common themes, we can begin to understand how past racial oppressions, which are not yet fully acknowledged, have become a permanent part of our national identity. Finally, we will explore the bishops' teaching on solidarity as an antidote to the lust to dominate. Conversion of our minds to justice requires that we listen to the experiences of those suffering due to racial injustice and that we align ourselves with them looking to a common future.

The Lust to Dominate

In pages 5–7 of the pastoral letter, the bishops challenge us to think about justice. This section reiterates the main themes of human dignity and shared identity as brothers and sisters united in Christ's love. Then it more explicitly connects human dignity with a just community. A just society "recognizes and respects the legitimate rights of individuals and peoples" (5). Human rights are rooted in each individual's theological identity because all of us are created in the image of God. By quoting Genesis 1:26-27 here, the bishops remind us that we are all children of God. This shared identity creates a moral obligation for us to live together without division or rank (1). Justice means being "in right relationship with God, with one another, and with the rest of God's creation" (6). The Holy Trinity provides us a powerful image for envisioning a just community. The bishops teach us that our human identity, like the Trinity, is to be persons-in-community. Twentieth-century theologian and mystic Howard Thurman wrote often about our fundamental moral obligation to foster community wherever we go. "We are created *for* community. We are born into community . . . and depend upon it for survival. We are nurtured by community. . . . Community is a gift of God. We honor this gift when we live in community with respect and care for its members and all creation."[1]

A just community includes everyone. In a just community, there are formal and informal safeguards for human dignity. We learn from each other how to respect other people and care for them. Laws and policies also should secure our expectations for the care and mutual support due to each and every member. Many of us have heard the expression: "Justice is what love looks like in public."[2] This means that our human relationships within the community must express our love for one another. Jesus' new commandment expands on our obligation to love, that we must love as God loves: "As I have loved you, so you also should love one another" (John 13:34). Love within a community of people is evident in the justice secured by its values, behaviors, laws, and aspirations.

Identifying community as the essence of our humanity means that the most damaging consequence of racism results when society excludes an entire group of people from membership with its joys and advantages. Instead of uniting people toward a shared future, racism pits people against one another, dividing them into "we" and "they." Moreover, racial privilege represents the power of one group to reject the humanity and worthiness of another group. Because racism is more than a simple insult, racial superiority is not just one sin among many. Instead, it is a particularly devastating sin because it sins against the community itself. It imposes widespread political, social, and economic consequences that last for generations.

> Racism imposes widespread consequences that last for generations.

We understand the story of Adam and Eve's "fall" as the primordial example of how people have rejected God's vision for creation as the dwelling place for human beings in community. The story narrates how the first human beings rejected God's generosity by choosing instead to live according to their own values. We can interpret this for ourselves as revealing the devastating costs when people prefer their own needs to living in loving relationships with God and with others. In the fourth century, St. Augustine called the lust to dominate the original sin of humanity. The story reveals the way we grasp and take what we want rather than receiving all good things that we need from God's graciousness. Our other sufferings and sins flow from this fundamental choice to prefer independent power over relationship in community. The bishops come directly to the point: "Whether recognized or not, the history of the injustices done to so many, because of their race, flows from this 'lust to dominate' the other" (6).

Racial Injustice as Lust to Dominate

Having set forth the theological foundation of human community as right relationship, Open Wide Our Hearts recounts how European Americans have dominated other racial groups. Rev. Luther Smith Jr. of Emory University explains this point clearly: "So many breakdowns in relationships among humans result from the urge to dominate others. The most blatant division within societies is between the privileged and the disinherited."[3] Our country's history is a vicious and disturbing story where we see how the lust to dominate has been, and continues to be, glorified in our cultural values. The victims of the lust to dominate are those who are disinherited. The antidote to the lust for power is empathy, which comes from deep listening and identifying with the sufferings of others. The bishops remind us: "We must create opportunities to hear, with open hearts, the tragic stories that are deeply imprinted on the lives of our brothers and sisters, if we are to be moved with empathy to promote justice" (7).

The histories of Native Americans, African Americans, and Hispanic Americans narrated in this letter provide only the briefest sketch of the centuries of racial injustice in our national past.[4] In the United States, we often proclaim proudly that we are a melting pot of diverse people. We pride ourselves on being a nation of immigrants. We understand our nation, at its best, as a place where all are equal, where all are welcome. But our history of racial and ethnic identity is so much more complex and fractured than a peaceful assimilation of strangers into a vibrant mixture of peoples, cultures, and values.

Nevertheless, the stories of stigmatized and oppressed groups in the letter can help us find ourselves in our nation's history of race. The lust to dominate is the history of everyone in our country, those who descend from the dominated and those who descend from the dominators because the history affects us all and distorts our culture even today. To understand how our common past still impacts the present, we must extend the discussion of racism from chapter 1.

The antidote to the lust for power is empathy.

Next we will explore the complexity of racial categories as they operate in our culture.

Stigma and Privilege

Racism has shifted its form over the centuries: from genocide and enslavement, to segregation and ghettos, to mass incarceration, to economic exclusion, and now to unjust deportations. One of the reasons that racism persists, the bishops write, is because we often try to ignore our past oppressions as no longer relevant: "The evil of racism festers in part because, as a nation, there has been very limited formal acknowledgment of the harm done to so many, no moment of atonement, no national process of reconciliation and, all too often a neglect of our history" (7).

If our goal is truly to eradicate racism, we must confront its reality as an insidious form of social stigma and privilege still with us. Even a century and a half after Lincoln issued the Emancipation Proclamation and sixty years after legal segregation ended with the Civil Rights Act and the Voting Rights Act, our culture still assigns value to human beings according to physical traits. Judging a person's color or race often includes making presumptions about their intelligence, moral character, or God-given talents, the "prejudice" that the bishops mention. But if we take a moment to reflect, we realize that these presumptions are completely unwarranted. There is no objective basis for connecting physical or observable features with a human being's talents and moral qualities.[5] Yet we do this all the time. For centuries in our country, skin color has carried legal and social significance, both negatively and positively.

"White" has been the so-called normal and positive quality. When we label someone as a race *other than white*, we stigmatize them and imply that they are not up to the standard. A stigma is a blemish or a mark of shame that reduces a person's humanity and often disqualifies them from full participation in society.[6] We can think of the lepers in Scripture, who were ostracized physically and socially. The lepers were condemned to live outside of the villages. This is why Jesus' healing touch both cured their disease and reunited them into society. Without the stigma of leprosy, they were welcomed back into the community. The crux of racial stigma is to link physical qualities (skin, hair, or facial/body features) with a lesser status in society or outright exclusion.

Although stigmas are essentially false stereotypes, they endure in a culture because they serve the interests of the dominant group. A stigmatized person feels shame and experiences a range of hardships. These hardships may include extreme stress, suspicion from the dominant group, loss of status, and diminished identity development (especially when the stigma is internalized). Stigmatization also means physical, economic, and political isolation with very real impact on people's life opportunities. Stigmatized people are often denied access to jobs, health care, education, voting rights, and even basic legal presumptions of innocence, moral integrity, and trustworthiness. People of the dominant group may disparage or ignore those who are stigmatized. They may overcompensate in interactions to obscure the awkwardness of cultural stigma. People of the privileged group may discriminate and exclude stigmatized people from social and economic advantages intentionally or unconsciously, simply by accepting the status quo.[7] Stigmas imposed on non-whites today are particularly oppressive because they perpetuate and repeat past exploitation, domination, and violence, but they appear to be no one's fault.

The flipside of stigma is privilege. When some are stigmatized for their skin type or other features, others are necessarily privileged for these same qualities. In a country whose founding document declares "all men are created equal," we often gloss over privilege and claim to be color-blind to avoid confronting the complex and difficult reality of racism.[8] White people might try to avoid the benefits of their privilege

Ignoring or denying racial privilege will not eliminate it.

and the disadvantage it places on others by not speaking about it. Ignoring or denying racial privilege will not eliminate it, because it is a "social inheritance." Social inheritance, like wealth and treasure, is passed from one member of a group to another, as Georgetown sociologist Dyson describes.[9] What he means is that white people get the benefits of their racial label (such as being presumed to be truthful or hardworking), regardless of whether they want them.

With this understanding of stigma and privilege, we can now explore how the expressions we use in our culture in fact help conceal privilege so that it is less noticeable. Our language actually conceals racism and makes it more difficult to address. The most frequent linguistic device is simply *not* to mention whiteness and white European culture but to take them for granted as shared by everyone. A quality that is presumed to be natural and always present becomes the measure or standard. It is presumed to be the case, which is why the characteristic does not even have to be mentioned.[10] Only deviations from the standard are noticed. Think, for example, of which hand you write with or use to throw a ball. We presume someone is right-handed, while we usually clarify that someone is a "lefty" (or "southpaw"). Unremarked qualities are statistically more common and frequently preferred. When we design spaces or manufacture items, the unremarked quality is presumed—for example, scissors that cut only when used with the right hand. In the same way, the unremarked social identity of a group indicates that this group is the standard according to which others are measured. People usually announce, explain, and label non-standard identities to show that they differ from what we otherwise expect and value.

Our racial categories are weighted toward a presumption of whiteness. Whiteness is taken for granted. It is literally *unremark-able*. Whenever we don't mention white identity or European ancestry, we obscure and preserve the advantage of whiteness

When we avoid mentioning racial identity, we neglect our history and the present reality of racism.

and the accompanying race-based stigmas for non-whites. Generally, only stigmatized (non-white) racial identities are noted. We can all recall news stories and media descriptions that explicitly mention race: "Ms. Smith, who is black, was stopped by the police today." But would we expect to hear: "Mr. Jones, a white man, is running for mayor of his hometown"? In the same vein, when white people describe themselves, very often they will not mention their skin color or racial identity. "White privilege means not having to say you are white."[11] It also means that white people do not have to acknowledge their social dominance. When we mention the racial identities of non-whites, the implicit message is that these identities are less valued, perhaps blemished or defective because they are not up to the standard.

We can see that it can be socially awkward for white people to recognize their whiteness because whiteness implies dominance and preference in a society that purports to value equality. People who are labeled white are often surprised when someone asks: "What race are you?" Their answers sometimes deflect or hide from claiming to be white; instead they might mention their specific European national ancestry. Maybe we can recall a time when a white person protested that he or she is not really any race, that race does not matter, or that he or she is "normal." These reactions fail to acknowledge racial privilege and stigma forthrightly. When we avoid mentioning racial identity, even with the best intentions, we neglect our history and the present reality of racism. This avoidance can be labeled complicity and interpreted as a deliberate decision to retain our positions of privilege and advantage.

The practice of concealing racism operates everywhere in our daily life. We even can see it in the way Open Wide Our Hearts conceals whiteness and white actors. As we read the section *Do Justice*, we might notice a strange writing construction—the passive voice. An easy example of passive voice in grammar is the difference between "the girl kicked the ball" (active voice) and "the ball was kicked" (passive voice). The passive voice identifies who receives the action (the ball), but the actor (the girl) is hidden. When narrating the experiences of various non-white groups in United States history, the letter uses passive voice. We know who is harmed, but not who inflicted the harm. For example, note the statement: "African Americans were disadvantaged by slavery, wage theft, 'Jim Crow' laws, and by the systematic denial of access to numerous wealth-building opportunities reserved for others" (11). Passive voice can make us feel that an action is unavoidable or simply unfortunate because the grammatical device hides the identity of the person or people who caused the injury.

However, we know from the bishops' own definition in Open Wide Our Hearts that racism is a feeling of superiority on the part of some combined with the actions they take to enforce that superiority. *Someone* must have stolen the wages, enacted the unjust laws, and denied African Americans access to economic safety. The unspoken actors are, of course, European Americans who as a racial group have benefitted by exploiting, exterminating, enslaving, and excluding people of other ethnicities and races.[12] How would we react if the bishops had written: "European Americans enslaved people from Africa and their descendants, stole their wages and their labor, and denied them opportunities for jobs, good housing, and adequate education"? Actually, they do eventually acknowledge that whites have oppressed others, but not until the final section of the pastoral letter.

Eradicating racism begins with understanding what racism is and how its categories work to expose and hide cultural oppression. Racial labels are not value-neutral descriptions in our country. Rather, through them we assign social judgments and award or deny privileges. We can listen now with open hearts to our own national history of racial injustice.

Listening to the Stories

Sounding again the themes of listening and conversion, *Do Justice* relates the experiences of three specific groups whose members have been killed, enslaved, exploited, and marginalized because of European Americans' lust to dominate. In a few cursory paragraphs, we hear the long history of misery and violence that each group experienced and the tears they shed. The histories lack extensive details, but we can still find several common themes. First, racial oppression and violence began when the Europeans first encountered indigenous people in Africa and the Western Hemisphere. Second, the exploitation and oppression have continued for centuries, although their form and impact have changed. Third, there are a few bright spots in these stories, people who have resisted racial injustice in small but significant ways. Let's connect the dots.[13]

The stories of Native Americans, African Americans, and Hispanic Americans reveal, first, a common theme of the Europeans' lust to dominate. The bishops' brief accounts display how European explorers and colonists viciously stole the lives, land, and liberty from the people already dwelling on this continent. The Europeans' arrival in the Western Hemisphere launched a centuries-long genocide and extermination of Native Americans through outright slaughter, land theft, broken treaties, forced relocation, and intentional annihilation of their tribal cultures and religions.[14] The experience of African Americans as an oppressed people began when Europeans kidnapped more than 12 million men, women, and children from Africa. The inhuman transatlantic slave trade lasted nearly three centuries. Enslaved Africans and their descendants worked the land occupied by European settlements and colonies throughout the Western Hemisphere until the late nineteenth century. The savagely violent institution of chattel slavery employed terrorism to subjugate and control the enslaved people. Chattel slavery was "far more brutal than the slavery known in ancient times," the bishops note, because it was an economic practice that stole the lives and futures of people in permanent servitude. "Families were separated, marriages were forbidden or dishonored, and children were maltreated and forced to work" (10). Open Wide Our Hearts also chronicles the history of people from the nation of Mexico, who live in what is now the southwestern United States. The United States seized their land and their homes in the Mexican-American War in the mid-nineteenth century, an act of imperialism and conquest by our young nation. The lust to dominate and the power to conquer were the very reasons Europeans were able to control the North American continent and become a world power in the twentieth century. Taken together, the bishops' examples identify a pattern at the heart of US culture that started even before we became a nation and continues in various guises even today.

Second, by reflecting on these stories we realize that European American exploitation of Native Americans, African Americans, and Hispanic Americans utilized similar mechanisms. While these tools of oppression have changed and vary from group to group, the common pattern remains: stigmatization of non-Europeans and securing privileges to those of European descent through law, custom, and force if necessary.[15] We learn from the pastoral letter that marginalized groups suffer poverty, poor health care, inadequate schools, social disparities, and political disenfranchisement even to today. We can recognize the lust to dominate alive and well in our inordinate national emphasis on individual success. When we make individual success and pursuit of money our primary values, we intentionally reject Christ's commandment to love one another. Placing the personal pursuit of success and achievement above care for other human beings yields tragic consequences for the people whose life and liberty we trample as we assert our individual freedoms.

Third, in these brief histories of racial oppression, the bishops raise up for us moments of good news. They name various missionaries who defended Native Americans' rights or who evangelized them (9). They list some of the religious orders that ministered to African Americans (11). Open Wide Our Hearts also names a handful of the holy men and women in these racial groups who lived the Gospel in a saintly way. They can be our models, and we may ask what their witness today can teach us as questions of racism and racial justice become more complex.

Part of our continuing conversion to racial justice will be to examine particular stories in more detail, so let's take one example now. Open Wide Our Hearts mentions Dr. Thomas Wyatt Turner, although without supplying much information about him. However, we know from other sources that he founded the Federated Colored Catholics (FCC) in 1924 "to develop a black voice for the concerns of black Catholics within their church," and to demand systemic and social transformation of US laws and culture.[16] These demands included better jobs to earn a decent livelihood, education for black children in Catholic schools, admission to Catholic institutions regardless of race, no more lynching, full citizenship and voting rights, and an end to presuming that blacks were a threat to whites. In short, the FCC was seeking more just treatment for blacks both in society and within the Catholic Church. However, historical sources record that the white Jesuit John LaFarge led a successful reformulation of the FCC because he believed that whites ought to lead in solving the "race problem." Massingale, author of *Racial Justice and the Catholic Church*, compares Turner's principles for advancing blacks' empowerment with the objectives of LaFarge and

> Solidarity overcomes our lust to dominate.

his colleagues. "The white resolutions have no call for systemic change. Rather they focus on treating black individuals with courtesy, decency, and respect. The contrast could not be more glaring: one approach advocates for social transformation; the other calls for good manners. One presses for justice; the other counsels kindness."[17] Because people with privilege can be unaware of its negative impact on others, all efforts to heal racism require that people who have been excluded and oppressed have a full voice in shaping an adequate response. Moreover, when we listen to the demands of people who have been wounded by racism, we practice the respect for human dignity that is due equally to all members of society along with the right to self-determination.

In this section of Open Wide Our Hearts, the bishops show us briefly that violence, extermination, and oppression constitute both a social legacy and a continuing sin. Our separate racial identities are culturally reinforced even in the present because benefits and burdens continue to be allocated along lines of race. We have "never sufficiently contended with the impact of overt racism" (13). The bishops call for solidarity because they realize that a single community in Christ has not yet been achieved in our nation. Solidarity overcomes our lust to dominate.

Conversion Begins with Solidarity

In closing, *Do Justice* repeats the bishops' urgent call to conversion that begins with open hearts. "Much can be learned in hearing the stories of those who have lived through the effects of racism. In examining the generational effects of racism on families, communities, and our Church, each of us can begin to act in solidarity to change the prospects for future generations" (13). In Catholic social thought, solidarity means that we align ourselves with the needs of others, especially those who are marginalized by social, legal, and cultural practices. Solidarity is the committed, intentional practice of seeing "the 'other'—*whether a person, people, or nation*—not just as some kind of instrument with a work capacity and physical strength to be exploited at a low cost and then discarded . . . but as our 'neighbor,' a 'helper'. . . to be made a sharer, on a par with ourselves [as equal members of a just community]."[18] Massingale's insights about the Federated Colored Catholics leadership show how paternalism undermines solidarity and vitiates the struggle for justice. Solidarity, like other Gospel values, is a prophetic stance against the distorted priorities of individualism and materialism embedded in US culture. It counteracts the lust to dominate. Solidarity requires us to shape our choices to achieve the full integral development of everyone in society: the weak and the strong, the marginalized, as well as the powerful. Solidarity begins with getting to know the situation of others. To do justice is to practice solidarity. We cannot claim to have hearts wide open in love if we do not develop in our own lives the practices of social justice.

We are beginning to understand that justice is love in action, but knowing that something is true does not make it happen. We must desire justice with all our hearts. Then we must take meaningful steps to create a more just society. The next section of the letter, *Love Goodness*, strives to create in our hearts a deeper love for justice as God's goodness lived in a community that welcomes all people.

To do justice is to practice solidarity.

Questions for Reflection

1. In order to test the idea of linguistic markers and stigma, can you think of human categories where one trait is taken for granted? Think about:

a. the choice to eat meat and the way that vegan items are noted on menus;
b. the presumed gender of certain professions, so that we are surprised to meet male nurses or women engineers; and
c. the expected ethnicity of certain professions when over 93 percent of stockbrokers and airline pilots are white.

What do you notice about the way you might link racial traits with character, education, and employment?
You might take the Implicit Bias Test, available online, and reflect on what it means about your own racial biases.

2. Can you recall a time where your own worldview or presumptions made you blind to what someone was telling you? For example, perhaps you have seen a mixed-race married couple together but had to clarify exactly how they were related when they were introduced to you. How did you realize when you made a mistake about someone because of the presumptions you attached to race? What can we practice to make us more attentive to how racial presumptions operate in our culture?

3. How did you react to the passages in the letter and this guide that suggest that our nation has achieved its global dominance through a pattern of racial violence and oppression, particularly by European Americans?

Questions for Study

1. Some sociologists have said that the main racial categories in our nation today are white, almost white, not-white, and never-white. What evidence do you have to agree and to disagree with this? What more do you need to know?

2. The bishops tell us: "We must create opportunities to hear, with open hearts, the tragic stories that are deeply imprinted on the lives of our brothers and sisters, if we are to be moved with empathy to promote justice" (7). Review the resource list at the end of this guide, and select two items to read that tell the histories of racial groups in the United States. Discuss what you are learning with someone from that group to hear how their experiences confirm, challenge, or extend what you have read.

Prayer through the Witness of Our Lives

Let our hearts be broken. We shall:
> Recite the names of people who have suffered and died from violence.
> Accompany the sorrowing communities.
> Comfort those who fear for their futures.

In all our encounters, let us be unstintingly compassionate.

Let our minds be shrewd. We shall:
> Study the research on guns, poverty, environmental harms, and migration.
> Probe the relationship between violence and oppression, and their roots in white supremacy and bigotry.
> Diagnose the problems of our nation with honesty and courage.

In all our inquiries, let us prophetically measure *what is* against *what ought to be.*

Let our voices be raised. We shall:
> Discuss violence in moments of disruption and moments of calm.
> Rail against our planet's destruction.

Hold lawmakers and gun manufacturers accountable.
Preach against violent ideologies, particularly those driven
      by hate and racism.
In our every declaration, let us call relentlessly for a humane
future, a future worth living for all people.

Let our lives count in the struggle for justice and peace.
    Let us build community wherever we go.
    Let us love, let us love, let us love.
    Let us be bearers of love.

3 Love Goodness
Converting Our Hearts

Let us turn now to the heart of the letter—how our love for God demands that we eradicate racism. We demonstrate our love for God in our love for each other. We hear again the commandment to "love goodness," and so we need to dig more deeply into the idea of love. Recall that the letter's prior section, *Do Justice,* ended with a call to solidarity after we listened to stories of oppression and injustice from our own history. Racism affects every person in the United States because racial categories are embedded in our social structures, our language, and our policies. As we deepen our understanding of racism, we also must convert our hearts so that our love bears fruit. Through our passion for racial justice we "change the prospects for future generations," and secure greater peace and well-being for our children and grandchildren (13).

Our love for God demands that we eradicate racism.

The section *Love Goodness* in the pastoral letter offers us the scriptural, theological, and moral guidance to form our consciences and convert our hearts (13–16). Let's consider first the guidance the bishops give us about loving goodness, reemphasizing the main themes of the letter. We will then discuss what social sin is and how it applies to racism. We will close this chapter by learning from Catholic social thought about solidarity. We love goodness when we embrace what goodness means in the realm of society and community.

The Call to Love in Scripture

"Each of us should examine our conscience," we hear the bishops saying (13). Examining our conscience means reflecting on our own thoughts and actions in light of what God calls us to do. In *Love Goodness*, the letter highlights three key Scripture passages that impart lessons about God's commandment to love one another. We notice in these passages how love brings harmony into community. Our failure to love ends in division and competition, which profoundly distorts our human relationships.

1. The letter quotes Matthew's gospel, where Jesus summarizes the essence of his message: "You shall love the Lord, your God, with all your heart, with all your soul, and with all your mind. This is the greatest and the first commandment. The second is like it: You shall love your neighbor as yourself" (Matt 22:37-39; referenced at 14). The love of God made visible is precisely the love of our neighbor, and every human being is our neighbor.

2. From the first chapter of Genesis, we read about Cain, who killed his brother Abel out of jealousy (Gen 4:3-16; referenced at 14). Cain and Abel forever symbolize the discord that led to the death of one brother and the social ostracism of the other.

3. Citing St. Paul's first letter to the Corinthians, the bishops highlight Christ as the model of love that heals every division (14). Above all, we recognize that Christ embraced

all people who were marginalized by social conventions, poverty, and religious dictates.

The bishops' message from scripture is that love is our path to eliminate the superiority-inferiority division, the we-they attitude, which marks the "core of racism." Citing Pope Benedict XVI, they assert that love "is an extraordinary force which leads people to opt for courageous and generous engagement in the field of justice and peace" (14, quoting *Caritas in Veritate* 1). Christ's love "binds together the Church" and "reaches out beyond the Church to all peoples. *This love also requires justice*" (14, emphasis added). Open Wide Our Hearts is inviting us to expand our understanding of love and to recognize that to love goodness means to seek justice in society.

This section closes with stories about two holy people from the nineteenth century who modeled love in order to resist racial injustice and foster racial reconciliation. The letter introduces Servant of God Augustus Tolton,[1] who was born into slavery in the mid-nineteenth century and ordained to the priesthood in Rome because seminaries in the United States refused to admit him. He suffered discrimination and torment at the hands of white clergy. During Tolton's faithful ministry in a black parish in Chicago, he "exhibited the love of Christ, forgiving what was done to him and continuing to serve others" (15). The letter invokes St. Katharine Drexel as a second example of service toward racial reconciliation. She worked among people in Native American and African American communities, "exhibiting genuine respect and concern," through education and other compassionate services (16). Her witness inspired more than 500 sisters during her lifetime to serve the needs of Native Americans and African Americans by founding the Sisters of Divine Providence. We recognize in Servant of God Tolton and St. Katharine Drexel two extraordinary figures of love. We can honor them as models of loving service and people who worked for racial reconciliation.

While loving people different from ourselves and caring for them through charity and tenderness are indispensable Christian virtues, there is more to consider here. As the bishops admonish: "This love [acting to eradicate racism] also requires justice" (14). Because racism is a social and cultural legacy, to eliminate the current injustices of racism and the impediments due to past oppressions our love must be more than charitable acts. That is, we must strive very intentionally for social justice as the publicly visible measure of our response to the call to love. Catholic social thought provides the foundation for connecting goodness and justice. For the remainder of this chapter, we will examine why our goodness must encompass justice if we hope to eradicate racism. This means we must refocus our attention from personal sin to social sin.

> To love goodness means to seek justice in society.

The Call to Love in a Situation of Social Sin

When we think of sin, we usually think of sin between two people. We think about physical and emotional injuries we inflict on others, usually through selfishness or pride. When Open Wide Our Hearts speaks of a call to love, the examples and teachings seem likewise to focus on personal assaults and indignities. Recall how Tolton forgave white clergy who humiliated him and refused to recognize his call to priesthood. This example directs our attention to individual actors, which is appropriate because only individuals can sin. However, if we only think of our obligation to love as direct kindness to another person, we will not be able to address the social injustice of racism, which is entrenched in our culture and values.

Sin is often described as a distortion, something wrong, in people's relationship with God and with each other. God does not create, cause, or desire sin. People sin, both as individuals and in groups, when they harm each other and refuse to live according to God's love. The Hebrew Scriptures provide a better image for social sin, which is the notion that our actions miss the mark. Social sin is not exactly the type of sin that is a direct offense to other people. Instead, social sin refers to the harmful consequences of individual sins that develop and accumulate over time. Our relationships may miss the mark not because of what we do, but because of what we fail to do and the way our lives together limit rather than give life. Recall here our discussions of culture from prior chapters. Our culture, rather than any specific activity or individual actor, perpetuates the injustice in our nation. So that we are not tempted to accept racism as individual acts of intolerance, we need a better understanding of social sin.

Consider, for example, a family where the father is an alcoholic. Perhaps he is abusive and physically violent. The children try to become invisible by being good and not upsetting him. They comply with his unreasonable demands. In order to shield her children from violence, the mother may deflect her husband's anger and suffer abuse and beatings herself. The family becomes isolated just to survive the next onslaught of mistreatment and to hide their shame. Instead of love, mistrust takes root in their hearts and governs their interactions. The children in this kind of family learn how violence gets them what they want. They may have few examples of true generosity and tenderness, so they do not even realize that there are better ways to get along with other people. The children may themselves grow up to be abusive parents. We can say that the original violence in the family creates the conditions for violence in the future. While the children when fully grown will be held accountable for their own choices to be violent, the consequences of their upbringing make loving others so tragically difficult. In the same way, the weight of individual and group sins makes it all the more likely that we will sin again and again. This is the condition described by the phrase *social sin.*

Like a dysfunctional family, racism is a social sin. Our current laws, social customs, and cultural values are racially unjust because of our four-hundred-year history of racial oppression and injustice. The racial injustice will inevitably continue even when well-intentioned people love and respect others. There are several points to note. First, the social sin of our culture is a real, historical, and continuing injustice. Second, our systemic racism is in some way unintentional. We inherit a system of cultural and religious symbols that legitimate unjust practices; we are forced to work within institutions and structures that often intensify harm. Our racially unjust culture and its institutions shape and constrain us without our consent. Third, a sinful culture implants in people a false assessment of their own worth. The people who are privileged by the culture can be unaware of its skewed values and how its rules and customs favor their success. Finally, dysfunctional cultures, like ours, are fractured and divided. As the bishops note, we think in terms of competing rather than complementary interests. Because of all of these factors, we often cannot even imagine what a racially just society could look like. The important point here is that racism is an unjust social condition that requires a social or society-based remedy. Our response to racism must include seeking justice.

> Our response to racism must include seeking justice.

Let's consider again the witness of Fr. Tolton, whom the bishops praise for forgiving his white detractors. Certainly, we honor the way he loved his enemies as an imitation of Christ. But we can learn something even more important about social sin from his situation. His courage to forgive whites who denied his human dignity was ineffective against systemic racism for two reasons. First, as an emancipated slave, his forgiveness had no power to effect legal remedies that other freed men and women needed to become full members of society. We never even learn whether his generosity changed the hearts of his oppressors. Second, his forgiveness may well have reinforced distorted cultural stereotypes that black people should be grateful and be encouraged to accept their ill treatment humbly as a trial from God. We might get the wrong message—that the holiest Christians will accept unjust suffering in an unredeemed society.

For these reasons, we must imagine what God's call to love looks like in a situation of social sin, such as the racism in our nation. Open Wide Our Hearts tells us that we must rectify an injustice in every way we can. The bishops remind us of our sins of omission, of what we fail to do. A sin of omission in our national situation is the passive acceptance of the racial status quo and the refusal to act to eradicate racial injustices. In the face of social sin, our personal sinfulness attaches when we know about a social injustice and fail to act. Therefore, our response to social sin entails personal actions that seek to create a more just culture, in addition to loving people in our daily encounters with them.

A Social Response to Social Sin

Open Wide Our Hearts reminds us that our call to resist racism through love "requires us to reach out generously to the victims of this evil, to assist the conversion needed in those who still harbor racism, and to begin to change policies and structures that allow racism to persist" (15). Racism emerged as the fundamental principal governing our social system in the United States as European American Christians sought to justify genocide and slaveholding. The sin of whites in the establishment of our country was to believe that their technologically more powerful culture was evidence of God's favor for them.[2] They then enacted laws to preserve their dominant social position and created social myths about the moral and intellectual inferiority of non-whites to justify mistreating and controlling them. So today racism "is not only a moral evil [as a failure to love], but a social sin maintained through systems of white privilege."[3] For this reason, our response must be designed specifically to eradicate the unjust systems and the distorted evaluations of racial groups that perpetuate the violence of racism.

In *Racial Justice and the Catholic Church*, theologian Bryan Massingale explains why racial healing must entail more than eliminating conflict among individuals and fostering goodwill.[4] First, he points out that when we focus on goodwill, we reduce the affirmative duty to love to mean that we should be friendly. To test this, we can recall our interactions with people of other racial groups. These might be purchases in a store, greetings and small talk with coworkers, or dining out. Upon reflection, most of us can honestly conclude that we have never said anything insulting or acted intolerantly to people of other races. Therefore, we might easily absolve ourselves of any duty to respond to the social sin of racism. But when we examine the quality of such exchanges, we find that they are mostly superficial and governed by customs of public courtesy. They are rarely meaningful encounters that affect someone's well-being or prospects for fulfillment in life.[5] Let's revisit the thought experiment from chapter 1, when we imagined how a privileged group shares employment benefits through social networks. Of course, friendship across racial boundaries can extend a person's network. But when we focus on *systems* of employment and hiring, we know that friendliness does not secure nondiscriminatory hiring processes. Positive conversations do not revamp employment development programs to equip job seekers with marketable skills.[6]

Instead, Massingale stresses the importance of a socially informed response to racism, which is the approach that we have

The social sin of racism demands a social response.

been working on in this guide. Because racism is a social phenomenon, we must begin with careful social analysis in order to eradicate it. This includes attending to the impact of cultural symbols, stigmas, language conventions, and locked-in racism in social patterns that form one generation after another until the colorized social order seems natural or else intransigent. He cautions that extended theological and ethical reflections demand honesty and humility, qualities that develop over long periods of prayerful conversation with God and one another. Even when we begin to grasp the magnitude of systemic racism, formulating an adequate response requires a deep and sustained commitment to radical change in the way we live together. Struggling for justice in the social and political realm, moreover, requires a formal, organized plan, tailored to the various levels and sectors of our community life. Racial injustice in the United States has lasted for centuries. Reconstructing our society and repairing these deep wounds obviously will require a long, long period of concerted actions. Massingale concludes that any plan to work for a more just society must learn from those who have suffered from injustice, especially in how they view the path toward equal empowerment so that we may overcome the legacies of oppression permanently. This means that one group cannot impose a solution upon another group, even as a matter of charity or goodwill. For all these reasons, the social sin of racism demands a social response.

Solidarity as Love Responding to Injustice

Throughout Open Wide Our Hearts, the bishops reiterate the call to love and the demand for solidarity. Solidarity has particular qualities that require us to act. Solidarity is best grasped within the whole context of Catholic social thought and the resources this tradition provides to us. We recall that the introduction to Open Wide Our Hearts makes these two important points: (1) to be created in the image of God as Trinity means that community life is necessary for individual life; and (2) we must love all people as brothers and sisters in Christ. Our Christian faith teaches us that living justly is actually countercultural in our nation, which idolizes the individual pursuit of wealth, property, and satisfaction. Our faith teaches us that justice in society is the practice of living through right relationships (6).

We can focus on two papal encyclicals written in the past fifty years to learn more about how love for others will foster a more just community and a more equal distribution of property, both of which are essential to racial justice. About community, we read St. John Paul II's encyclical letter on the hundredth anniversary of *Rerum Novarum* (*Centesimus Annus*), reminding us that societies are more than a collection of people.[7] He instructs us: "From the Christian vision of the human person there necessarily follows a correct picture of society" (CA 8). People dwell in living, organic communities, where they share identities, aspirations, and values. Communities are the source of individual life; just communities foster just and loving people. In *Laudato Sì*, Pope Francis also highlights the truth that human beings live in "intertwined relationships" with other human beings, as well as with God and creation (LS 66). He uses the idea of integral ecology to mean that everything is connected to everything else. Because our economic choices, culture, and daily lives have intersected to create our current ecological crisis, healing the earth as well as our relationships will require an integrated vision of reality across social, economic, moral, and political domains. The message of Catholic social teaching, then, is that the conversion of our hearts toward racial justice and reconciliation requires us to have a humble and generous view of ourselves as intimately intertwined with the lives of all other people. Our moral allegiance can no longer be to personal ancestries and particularized values, but our identity must first be forward looking—toward our shared future as brothers and sisters united through Christ's love.

These two encyclicals also alter our understanding of personal property. Catholic social thought links property to community in the idea of "common good." Common good refers to what is necessary for both individuals and society to thrive in an intertwined and life-giving way. *Centesimus Annus* is instructive here on property rights. The "universal destination of the earth's goods" means that no one can be excluded from the goods of creation (CA 6). It is immoral for people to seek unlimited wealth because this rejects our Catholic understanding that God created the world for all human beings. This has become known as the "universal destination of good." When we embrace the idea that people can seek unlimited personal wealth, we are rejecting the Catholic teaching that all people are entitled to share equitably in God's creation. Pope Francis sounds the same theme in *Laudato Sì*, teaching that the world and all creation belong to God, who bestows the goods of the world on all people. These encyclicals expose a second social sin in US culture, one related to racism. We sanction greed, over-consumption, and hoarding wealth. Severe economic disparity intersects with racial marginalization. If we were to respect the universal destination of goods as a matter of just practices, we would also reverse racism and alleviate its most pernicious impacts. So, we see that racial justice also demands a fair distribution of goods, including both tangible and intangible benefits and burdens in our community. Doing justice "is not merely a matter of giving from one's surplus, but of helping entire populations who are presently excluded or marginalized, to enter into the sphere of economic and human development" (CA 58).

> Severe economic disparity intersects with racial marginalization.

Goodness understood as justice makes a powerful and clear claim on us. Goodness understood as justice demands a prophetic reordering of our values. A just society assures that goods, opportunities, and well-being are available to all people, not just those with wealth and privilege (CA, part IV).[8] With our national history of racial oppression and exclusion, loving goodness means taking concrete actions to reorganize our society to include those who have been excluded, to heal past wounds and repair past losses, and to secure the future of every person. The test of our solidarity will be whether we create a just and equitable community for people of all backgrounds and heritages.

Speaking Practically

In this section *Love Goodness*, the bishops have led us to a socially complex understanding of justice as solidarity. Solidarity means we are one community; loving goodness means we are committed to fostering one *just* community. With hearts converted to justice, we still struggle with how to create a future radically different from our past. Practical steps will command our attention in the next chapter, *Walk Humbly with God*, as we strive to convert our actions so that they concretely demonstrate our love for justice.

Questions for Reflection

1. Can you find examples in your experience of the difference between offering someone goodwill and acting justly for their interests? Recall the saying: "Give a man a fish, and you feed him for a day. Teach a man to fish and you feed

him for a lifetime." How can this insight help us convert our hearts from charity to justice in our racially unjust society?

2. Consider the communities that you belong to. What makes you feel a part of these groups? How do people in communities behave toward each other? What claims can members of the same community make on each other?

Questions for Study

1. Read *Letter from Birmingham Jail* by the Reverend Dr. Martin Luther King Jr. (available online at https://kinginstitute.stanford.edu/king-papers/documents/letter-birmingham-jail).

   • What are the sources (scriptural, legal, or political) that he draws on for his argument? What does he say about personal action? What does he say about advocating for social and political change?

2. Recall that the saints are conditioned by their own culture but often are canonized by Catholic communities centuries later. Investigate one contemporary person who is fighting for racial justice in your city or state. What is their motivation? What is their vision for a more just future in our nation?

Prayer for Light and Courage

Blessed are you, God of the universe. We long for a just peace in society and among peoples, but our designs for achieving human community always reflect our own interests, and our efforts fall short. We read your will in Jesus' ministry, but it is hard for us to recognize the effects of your grace in our own actions. The values of your rule shine in the logic of life acted out by Jesus and taught in his words, but we are helpless in following the ways he walked. We need light and courage.

Gracious God, giver of all good things, we ask enlightenment to know how to apply the ideals of your rule. Illumine the paths that will lead us out of our darkness. Bless us with deeper visions and more penetrating sight so that we may apply Jesus' wisdom to our societies and find ways out of our frustration.

Gracious God, giver of all good things, we pray for courage to move our heavy limbs. In the power of your Spirit, push us to decisions that will be efficacious. With the impulse of your grace lift up and support our actions that we may sustain them to the end. Turn our desires outside ourselves, carry them in your love, and bring them decisively to the realization of your kingdom in our world and communities.

Come, blessed One, and bless our freedom. May your will be done on earth.
Amen.[9]

4 Walk Humbly with God
Converting Our Actions

We have now arrived at the final section of Open Wide Our Hearts with a deeper understanding of racial injustice in our nation. Our understanding needs to continue to expand as we pay attention to the racial sins in our culture and our own lives. But we cannot stop with understanding. From now on we must *walk humbly with God*, which means embodying racial justice in our lives. The actions that we must take are nothing short of revolutionary. The bishops write: "Racism is a moral problem that requires a moral remedy—a transformation of the human heart—that impels us to act" (16). When they define racism as a moral problem they mean that we can scarcely respond because we are not even able to judge the immorality of our own actions. Many of us lack a moral compass that is a reliable and trustworthy guide for this complex social sin, which pervades every aspect of our national and individual lives.

Therefore, responding to racism as a moral problem requires our comprehensive and sustained attention directed to upend everything we understand about our shared human identity. As we "walk humbly with God" according to the title of this section, we feel the challenge to leave behind racial categories that divide us and to repair the injuries caused by centuries of racial injustice. Building upon hearts converted to loving justly, we must

convert our actions as well. We must become a new community
of brothers and sisters in Christ. The vision of a new community
must also provide the leaven to help establish racial justice more
fully in our national culture. Creating a new community and new
structures to safeguard the dignity and well-being of each and
every person requires inspired moral imagination, courageous
conviction, and decisive action.

Because developing a completely new orientation to human
identity is daunting, the bishops offer directives and guidelines. They anticipate that their actions and ours
as Catholics will have an amplified effect the
more we practice true community without
racial divisions. They set the expectations for
the US Catholic Church when they solemnly
declare: "As bishops, we commit ourselves to
the following actions with the hope that others, especially those in our spiritual care, will do
likewise in their own lives and communities" (17). The final
section of Open Wide Our Hearts mixes teaching on faith
with recommendations and the bishops' promises for their
own activities. The theological and spiritual call remains the
same—conversion and action. That is, the bishops repeatedly
remind us of our obligation to love all people as brothers and
sisters in Christ

> The actions that we must take are nothing short of revolutionary.

Let's now consider specifically the plans that the bishops
endorse. As we read *Walk Humbly with God*, we notice that this
longer section is segmented under headings comprising two or
three paragraphs each. Instead of taking these one by one, we
will break them down by the groups they address. Our discussion will be organized by what the bishops themselves will do
to eradicate racism, what Catholic associations and groups
should do, and what all Catholics are called to do, especially
individuals.

The Bishops' Actions and Promises

The bishops have taken the following steps toward racial justice through this letter itself. In the very first section, "Acknowledging Sin," they admit that they have not led more decisively in the past to speak out and fight against racism. Their confession is important to quote here in full:

> Therefore we, the Catholic bishops in the United States, acknowledge the many times when the Church has failed to live as Christ taught—to love our brothers and sisters.[1] Acts of racism have been committed by leaders and members of the Catholic Church—by bishops, clergy, religious, and laity—and her institutions. We express deep sorrow and regret for them. We also acknowledge those instances when we have not done enough or [we have] stood by silently when grave acts of injustice were committed. We ask for forgiveness from all who have been harmed by these sins committed in the past or in the present. (18)

Obviously, this single apology for the centuries of violence and oppression in our nation does not eradicate the past. Still, it is noteworthy. Confession, particularly the institutional church's public confession, is a necessary step toward moral and social reform (17–18). As in the sacrament of reconciliation, as a first step to new lives, we must confess our sins and resolve to sin no more.

We hear the letter praised and critiqued in the media, in homilies, and in Catholic schools. Some people both inside and outside the church wonder if the bishops' confession has any integrity and whether their actions will match their words. "No words, no matter how eloquently and enthusiastically uttered, can replace the expressiveness of action. Indeed, words become true when they are lived."[2] In addition to the words of confession, the bishops specify actions that are designed to make amends for the past. We can expect that the bishops will act consistently with their confession and that their actions will contribute to healing the racial divisions in our nation according to the church's social location and influence.

In "Resolving to Work for Justice," the bishops identify the specific responsibilities of the USCCB's Ad Hoc Committee Against Racism, which drafted Open Wide Our Hearts. This committee is tasked comprehensively to "facilitate an ongoing national dialogue," to "foster reconciliation, and publicly witness" for the church's commitment to ending racism, and to "advocat[e] for equality" in social policy and government spending (19–20).[3] The bishops pledge to support parish plans and initiatives relating to education and training parish ministries about racial justice, particularly in financially disadvantaged parishes (19–20). They promise to celebrate the diversity of the church, both past and present, by acknowledging particularly the identities and contributions of groups often hidden in our history. They will promote vocations among these communities (23). Finally, they commit themselves to provide the tools and resources needed to assist parishes' efforts toward racial healing and justice (22–23). In the short time since Open Wide Our Hearts was issued, the USCCB has already created a repository of materials to understand and address issues in the fight against racism.[4]

The real question will be how our church, including all of its members, organizations, and the bishops themselves, follow through with our change of heart. Will this acknowledgment of sin lead to the eradication of racism beginning with our actions now? Will this plan actually contribute to widespread efforts

> The real question will be how our church follows through with our change of heart.

toward racial justice that seem to be taking hold in our country? As Catholics we might sit back and nod mumbling, "Time will tell." However, the thrust of Open Wide Our Hearts is personal conversion. When we receive the bishops' confession and hear their plans, our moral obligation is to hold them accountable and to support the church's conversion by our own new commitments. When we take seriously the pastoral directives for Catholic groups and for individuals, which we will now discuss, we animate the conversion of the whole church toward racial justice.

Actions for Catholic Organizations and Groups

The bishops mandate specific actions for organizations and individuals working in parishes. These directives mostly relate to the various partners involved in Catholic education and formation. The institutions include parish religious education programs, diocesan schools and those sponsored by religious congregations, and Catholic seminaries and universities. People who lead education programs are required to respond, especially teachers and Catholic theologians and those who provide educational materials, such as Catholic media and publications, and all parish and organizational staff members, whether they are lay, ordained, or religious. In short, wherever and however Catholics meet for worship, formation, or education, we are charged with "developing and supporting programs that help repair the damages caused by racial discrimination" (22). Catholic institutions and their leaders cannot shy away from addressing the moral and pastoral aspects of racial injustice.

We can look at two examples of how to implement the guidelines in Open Wide Our Hearts. First, a parish or organization might examine its own historical engagement with marginalized groups. We can find a significant example in the process through which the Society of the Sacred Heart has confronted its history of slaveholding in Grand Coteau, Louisiana, in the nineteenth century.[5] In 2016, the congregational leadership created a Committee on Slavery, Accountability and Reconciliation that was charged to uncover the truths of the enslaved persons' stories in order to honor their memories and heal relationships. Over the course of two years, the congregation identified the descendants of people enslaved at the convent and dialogued with them about how to acknowledge this sin and recognize the enslaved persons. The reconciliation has so far included a memorial ritual, which descendants planned and attended, a monument with the names of the enslaved persons, a plaque marking the slave quarters and those who lived there, and plans for a museum at the school so that the history will not be forgotten. The work of reconciliation and healing continues with the congregation and the descendants of the people enslaved by their community generations ago.

A second path to educate and form ourselves to be more sensitive to racial justice and reconciliation can be simpler but just as intentional.[6] We can consistently include racial justice as a topic within regular programs or create specific discussions to explore our own situations. For example, Dr. Henry Fortier, the superintendent of the Catholic schools in the Diocese of Orlando, spoke to educators on "The Responsibility of Catholic Schools and Churches to Talk about Racism" as an immediate and direct response to Open Wide Our Hearts when it was published. In the same vein, Santa Clara University hosted a two-year faculty collaborative to reflect on justice, titled *Powering Forward Toward Racial and Ethnic Justice in Our Common Home.*[7] There were public presentations and discussions by experts and all materials have been made available on the university's website. Many other universities and

> The most important thing is for us to do *something.*

dioceses have undertaken similar initiatives. The most important thing is for us to do *something*. Taking small steps every week, every year, is better than planning a big program and hoping for huge impact.

We expect that Catholic organizations and institutions will comply with the directives in Open Wide Our Hearts, and as individual Catholics we must demand that they do. We can ask our pastors to preach against racism and to invite guest homilists to provide multiple perspectives on this social sin. We can initiate activities within our parishes and schools to educate ourselves and others. We can take social justice advocacy seriously by joining with local organizations that represent the interests of people of color who are marginalized by our society. We can offer community space to groups who can make us more aware of how racism distorts people's lives. Catholic organizations have their own sphere of influence in our nation, which we must claim as part of an authentic commitment to eradicate racism.

Actions for All Catholics

In *Walk Humbly with God*, we also find several directives that apply to all Catholics. We are called to resist racism through personal growth in three ways: by listening to others' experiences, by educating ourselves, and by examining our personal thoughts and actions. While these actions sound simple, they are not. First, the bishops ask us to be open to new situations and relationships. We are called to "[open] our minds and hearts to value and respect the experiences of those who have been harmed by the evil of racism" (19). This speaks most directly to people of privilege. The directive asks all of us to listen to and credit the experiences of those stigmatized and oppressed by racist structures and practices. People of color regularly experience suspicion and stereotyped judgments imposed on them because of our cultural stigmas. White people are often unaware of these daily trials.

Consider "driving while black," which captures the experience of African American drivers whom police stop without any justifiable concern, or think about Asian Americans, whose families have been citizens of the United States for generations, who are challenged, "No. Where are you *really* from?" People of European descent rarely experience such stigmatized scrutiny, nor must they routinely defend themselves as "real" Americans. Heightened scrutiny can lead to deadly outcomes, as when George Zimmerman shot and killed teenager Trayvon Martin in southern Florida. Racially biased scrutiny can also lead to the accumulating fears and anxieties carried by immigrants to our country regardless of their legal status. As we discussed in the first two chapters, the invisibility of whiteness carries the privileged presumption of innocence and normalcy. White people presume others are exaggerating and misinterpreting these challenging encounters or, worse, blame people of color for bringing the scrutiny on themselves.

The bishops remind us that we must listen *and believe* the experiences of people who are denied basic presumptions about their own goodness and respectability.[8] As a community committed to eliminating racial injustice, we can never avoid speaking about the harmful and painful impact of our racial biases. We must all be frank about the harm that racial stigma and oppression have on our brothers and sisters. By sharing personal narratives, people of color can teach whites about maintaining personal dignity and integrity despite assaults from others who would demean our humanity. If white people do not hear such stories, they too easily assume that we are a post-racial society. We are not. The dialogue of true encounter will require generosity and

> We are bound together in a future that we are creating now.

courage from those who share their experiences, humility from those who listen, and the shared hope of all for a better future to keep us going.

A second concrete response the bishops recommend to all of us is to "forg[e] authentic relationships" with people of all different backgrounds (19).[9] Beyond chatting at work or offering a greeting at Mass, a real relationship means friendship nurtured through shared life events. Friends comfort one another in sorrows and rejoice in each other's triumphs. Authentic relationships mean intimacy and mutual care as in any committed relationship. Real relationships are seen in the way we "have each other's back" by standing up for one another. It means recognizing that we are bound together in a future that we are creating now.

Authentic relationships across racial boundaries are rarer than we might think. Take for example a statistical study published in the *Washington Post* a few years ago. Research showed that "in a 100-friend scenario, the average white person has 91 white friends; one each of black, Latino, Asian, mixed race, and other races; and three friends of unknown race. The average black person, on the other hand, has 83 black friends, eight white friends, two Latino friends, zero Asian friends, three mixed race friends, one other race friend and four friends of unknown race."[10] People easily overestimate how many friends they have of different races and how meaningful the relationships are. We find, unfortunately, that living in integrated communities or studying in integrated schools will not dislodge people's fundamental cultural value that whiteness is superior. The numerous examples of whites wearing blackface show that our cultural conditioning and values are diabolically intractable. We can recall recent instances of blackface, such as Poly Prep Country Day School in Brooklyn, New York, and the Virginia governor's college photo, which included someone dressed in a KKK robe.[11] A little bit of conversation will not alter entrenched stigmas that have shaped our language, relationships, and political and social structures.

Rather, forging authentic relationships means our full-scale commitment to other people to share as much as possible their experiences and perspectives. Authentic relationships are nothing less than love made visible in our communities. We can learn about community and deep relationships from someone like Jean Vanier, founder of L'Arche International, who created homes for people with and without intellectual disabilities to live in common. In *Community and Growth: Our Pilgrimage Together*, Vanier writes that love is the foundation of community. "Love is neither sentimental nor a passing emotion. It is an attraction to others [that] gradually becomes commitment, the recognition of covenant, of a mutual belonging. . . . And if love means moving towards each other, it also and above all means moving together in the same direction, hoping and wishing for the same things."[12] In terms of encountering others and relationships across group boundaries, Vanier's advice means that the commitment to authentic relationships cannot be fleeting. We must make a wholehearted commitment to racial reconciliation by taking meaningful steps toward mutual belonging with sincere respect and care. If we belong to one another as sisters and brothers in Christ, our common lives must show this.

Imagining Racial Reconciliation

When Open Wide Our Hearts advocates for eradicating racism, we face a significant problem because we lack a shared understanding of what our society should look like. We might think about "racial reconciliation" and in this guide we have used the words "racially just society." There are also looming questions about making reparations for past injuries and thefts, such as paying damages to the descendants of enslaved people, compensating migrants across our southern border for illegal detentions and unjust wages, or returning ancestral lands to Native American Indian tribes. These are neuralgic issues that quickly drive wedges between people in communities. Instead we can look to experts for guidance.

In terms of racial reconciliation, Bryan Massingale identifies several questions for us to consider together in dialogue with others.[13] He asks us to imagine what the United States would be like without the stain of racism. Would the composition of our schools, workplaces, and organizations have proportionate membership from all racial groups? What would it feel like *not* to categorize people by race? What would it feel like positively to embrace racial differences and honor the distinctive cultures and qualities of racial groups? As we have done elsewhere in this guide, thought experiments that invite us to imagine a different future can be a really powerful tool in helping us know why and how we should change our actions.

After reflecting on these questions to help us envision the future, consider the following four dimensions of action required for interracial justice.[14] First, *recognition* requires that we acknowledge the historical and cultural roots of racial injustice. Other nations have used "truth and reconciliation" hearings to ensure that the there is an honest and full examination of the past.

> Imagine what the United States would be like without the stain of racism.

Next, *responsibility* means that groups accept their roles in causing racial wounds. Then, *reconstruction* entails taking active steps to heal psychological, social, and even physical wounds from past and present injustices. Finally, *reparation* refers to rectifying the material consequences due to whites' past oppression of other groups and current systemic advantages. Reparations, also known as affirmative redress, are the specific actions that make apologies real and effective. While many of these steps are beyond the scope of parishes and Catholic organizations, the church as a whole and all its members must come to terms with all the elements necessary for eradicating racism and the legacy of its wounds. We are wise to educate ourselves on these issues and to be ready to engage in these conversations if we are committed to a future where we are truly united in love as sisters and brothers in Christ.

Conversion and the Future

Open Wide Our Hearts closes with a final entreaty to our hearts. The bishops have charged Catholic organizations and individuals with definite initiatives to advance the fight for racial justice. They have committed themselves to actions on many fronts. Speaking about the long-term remedy of "Changing Structures," the bishops tell us: "The roots of racism have extended deeply into the soil of our society. Racism can only end if we contend with the policies and institutional barriers that perpetuate and preserve the inequality—economic and social—that we still see all around us. With renewed vigor, we call on the members of the Body of Christ to join others in advocating and promoting policies at all levels that will combat racism and its effects in our civic and social institutions" (23). They remind us that we must join with other religious traditions and social action groups to "repair the breach caused by racism, which damages the human family" (24). They invoke the vision of a united community where, "Going Forward," those harmed by racism may be healed (25–26).

Some people might see these actions as burdensome or unnecessary, but they are not heavier than the oppressions and harms borne by those enslaved, killed, excluded, or marginalized because of their physical attributes or place of origin. The magnitude of our sin impels us as a Catholic community to seek justice

We make ourselves who we are by how we act.

for our brothers and sisters. Still, it is tempting to be cynical about the possibility of ever eradicating racism, which has haunted our nation for centuries. People of color harmed by racism and oppression have often heard apologetic words and good intentions without experiencing any real relief or healing. But there is reason for hope. Human choices created our distorted culture. Therefore, human beings can change their cultures. We need to remember that we are self-constituting—we make ourselves who we are by how we act. We can recreate our society by our deliberate choices.

Like learning anything new, learning to eradicate racism demands that we grasp how racial injustice is rooted in our society and in our personal values and actions. We must be open to new perspectives and practice new behaviors. It is up to us individually and collectively to ensure that unjust structures are dismantled and that wounds are healed. This work is our responsibility as people who know in our hearts that all people are created in the image of God. All of us.

Questions for Reflection

1. What actions toward racial healing and eliminating racism will be easiest for you to try? Which will be hardest? Why?

2. Consider the bishops' commitments in *Walk Humbly*. In what ways is their commitment motivating for you? In what ways are their plans discouraging? How can you support the US Catholic Church's commitment to make racial justice a respect for life issue, in the same way that it has advocated against abortion and the death penalty?

Questions for Study

1. With a small group, read through the stories about George-town University's concerted efforts to repair the damage it inflicted on the enslaved African families it sold in 1838 to secure the college's financial security. What do you notice about:
   - the process of learning about the past injustices?
   - the people involved and their various perspectives and agendas?
   - the process of discernment about how to heal the community from past wounds—and the short- and long-term impact of these actions?

2. How might you explore what your parish and/or your organization has done to raise awareness and break your silence on racism, as the bishops recommend on page 22?

3. What process might you and your organization use to intensify your shared commitment to racial justice? Consider the Pastoral Circle that asks us to address a social issue through four steps: experience, analyze, reflect, and act (or sometimes more simply stated as *see-judge-act*). One example of the Pastoral Circle can be found at the Sisters of Saint Joseph of Peace website: https://csjp.org/peace-through-justice/the-pastoral-cycle/. How can you put the Pastoral Circle into practice as you discern how you are called to work for racial healing?

Prayer: Prophets of a Future Not Our Own

It helps, now and then, to step back and take a long view.
The kingdom is not only beyond our efforts, it is even beyond our vision.

We accomplish in our lifetime only a tiny fraction of the
    magnificent enterprise that is God's work. Nothing
    we do is complete, which is a way of saying that the
    Kingdom always lies beyond us.

No statement says all that could be said.
No prayer fully expresses our faith.
No confession brings perfection.
No pastoral visit brings wholeness.
No program accomplishes the Church's mission.
No set of goals and objectives includes everything.

This is what we are about.
We plant the seeds that one day will grow.
We water seeds already planted, knowing that they hold future
    promise.
We lay foundations that will need further development.
We provide yeast that produces far beyond our capabilities.
We cannot do everything, and there is a sense of liberation in
    realizing that.
This enables us to do something, and to do it very well.

It may be incomplete, but it is a beginning, a step along the
    way, an opportunity for the Lord's grace to enter and do
    the rest.
We may never see the end results, but that is the difference
    between the master builder and the worker.
We are workers, not master builders; ministers, not messiahs.
We are prophets of a future not our own.
Amen.[15]

Conclusion

We have studied Open Wide Our Hearts section by section. We can now consider it as a whole. As we close our study, we may step back to see our path, what we have learned, and what is next.

The pastoral letter represents another more direct and urgent message from the bishops in our nation to call us to be more just people in a more just society. The main theme of the letter is conversion. The bishops challenge all of us as Catholics in the United States to convert our minds, hearts, and actions to eradicate racism. The commitment to interracial justice is anchored in our shared human identity as people created in the image of God. Thus, we are all brothers and sisters united in Jesus Christ, which means we cannot rest until all people are respected and cared for in our society. Our work will not be finished until all people are vouchsafed the same opportunities, same respect, and same dignity in our nation. Throughout this study, we have repeatedly recognized that our fundamental faith commitment to justice in society is easier to express than to live.

Much of our discussion has been didactic—that is, we have learned *about* various topics relating to race, racial oppression, and racial justice. Learning about something, however, is a far cry from learning it and taking it to heart. We cannot stop with reading about the events of racism. Instead we must learn from our experiences in the world to recognize racial injustice at play.

> Conversion of our hearts and minds will take time, humility, and courage.

We must talk about what we experience and hear from others about what they notice and how they feel. We must absorb and reflect about how this sin distorts our nation today, including the very real legacies of past wounds. Only in this way may we move from head knowledge to knowledge of the heart. Most importantly, our hearts will be converted to love and enflamed by a passion to eradicate racism when we accept the reality of racism as our shared past. We begin the journey toward racial justice when we mourn for our own suffering and the suffering of our fellow human beings and embrace our responsibility to create a better future for all in the generations to come.

We have so far to go toward achieving racial reconciliation in the beloved community that Jesus call us to. Along the way, we will surely blunder. Our conversations will almost certainly be awkward and very likely painful. But we must ask forgiveness and try again, just as we do with the people we love most intimately. The bishops' apology in Open Wide Our Hearts models for us the humility to acknowledge that our past efforts have been inadequate. Conversion of our hearts and minds will take time, humility, and courage. New actions may seem inconsequential, but they will become significant and far-reaching when they are grounded in a profound awareness of our sins and a deep desire to change our culture and ourselves.

Above all, we need divine help. Through God's grace, the love of Jesus, and the fellowship of the Holy Spirit to lead us, we can strive to be released from the deadly fetters of racism into a life-giving community of justice. We pray seeking the intercession of Mary our Mother, all the saints, and all people of goodwill throughout the ages who have struggled for justice. We join our hearts and link our arms yearning for a future where all people are welcomed into a community of love.

Litany for Racial Justice

Wise and loving God,
you have created, and are still creating,
a world rich with difference and diversity.
You have created all people in your image,
each expressing their being and living their life
in special relationship with you—
  For all this, we give you praise.

For historical acts of injustice and oppression
perpetuated in our nation by our ancestors
against the First Nations people,
against people kidnapped from Africa and all their
    descendants,
against people who have traveled here from other continents,
Asia, Europe, Africa, and the Americas seeking a better life—
  Forgive us, merciful God.

For the times we have failed to recognize racism
in ourselves, in our church, in our society,
and the times we have failed to take action—
  Forgive us, long-suffering God.

For complicity in systems of privilege and power
over those whose skin color, culture, or creed
differ from the majority, even today—
  Forgive us, compassionate God.

Grant us patience in enduring periods of non-action,
persistence in resisting the evil of racial oppression,
and faithfulness in working toward racial justice
among your people in the church, and in the world—
  We beseech you, God of hope.

And grant us humility and wisdom to discern
when it is that your Spirit must come to accomplish
that which human beings and groups cannot.

We pray in the name of Jesus, himself,
the bread of justice and the cup of solidarity. Amen.[1]

Notes

Introduction

1. Unless otherwise noted, all parenthetical citations are page references to United States Conference of Catholic Bishops, *Open Wide Our Hearts: The Enduring Call to Love—A Pastoral Letter Against Racism* (Washington, DC: USCCB, 2018). Katharine Drexel's statement is cited at footnote 30: "A Eucharistic Focused Mission," Sisters of the Blessed Sacrament, http://www.katharinedrexel.org/wp-content/uploads/2016/11/FocusedMissionBro.pdf.

2. USCCB, "U.S. Bishops Approved 'Open Wide Our Hearts: The Enduring Call to Love, A Pastoral Letter Against Racism,'" news release, November 14, 2018, http://www.usccb.org/news/2018/18-186.cfm.

3. United States Catholic Conference, Brothers and Sisters to Us: U.S. Bishops Pastoral Letter on Racism (Washington, DC: USCC, 1979), http://www.usccb.org/issues-and-action/cultural-diversity/african-american/brothers-and-sisters-to-us.cfm.

4. For background on Catholic social teaching through 2005, see Kenneth R. Himes, Lisa Sowle Cahill, Charles E. Curran, David Hollenbach, and Thomas A. Shannon, *Modern Catholic Social Teaching: Commentaries and Interpretations* (Washington, DC: Georgetown University Press, 2005).

5. See David Cloutier, *Reading, Praying, Living Pope Francis's Laudato Si: A Faith Formation Guide* (Collegeville, MN: Liturgical Press, 2015).

6. USCCB, "U.S. Bishops Approved, *supra* at 2."

7. USCCB, "U.S. Bishops Approved."

8. National Conference of Catholic Bishops Committee on African American Catholics, Love Thy Neighbor as Thyself: U.S. Bishops Speak against Racism (Washington, DC: NCCB, 2001), http://www.usccb

.org/issues-and-action/cultural-diversity/african-american/upload/14 -026-love-thy-neighbor.pdf.

9. Debby Irving, "Finding Myself in the Story of Race: Debby Irving: TEDx Fenway," July 20, 2015, video, 15:18, https://youtu.be/oD5Ox5XNEpg.

Chapter 1

1. Margaret Guider, "Moral Imagination and the *Missio Ad Gentes*: Redressing the Counterwitness of Racism," *Proceedings of the Catholic Theological Society of America* 56 (2001): 54.

2. See Eduardo Bonilla-Silva, *Racism without Racists: Color-Blind Racism and the Persistence of Racial Inequality in America*, 4th ed. (Lanham, MD: Rowman & Littlefield, 2014), which details the racially discriminatory impact of policies and practices that appear to be neutral according to their plain language. For example, anyone can put money into a tax-deferred 529 Education Fund, but in reality this tax-savings maneuver mostly benefits wealthier people, those who have extra income to put toward long-term personal and family savings. The author demonstrates that our nation has not become the color-blind society we claim we are.

3. For background information on cultural analysis, see Andrew Milner and Jeff Browitt, *Contemporary Cultural Theory: An Introduction*, 3rd ed. (London: Routledge, 2013).

4. Bonilla-Silva, *Racism without Racists*, 9.

5. Brian Thompson, "The Racial Wealth Gap: Addressing America's Most Pressing Epidemic," *Forbes* (February 18, 2018), https://www.forbes .com/sites/brianthompson1/2018/02/18/the-racial-wealth-gap-addressing -americas-most-pressing-epidemic/. Wealth measures a family's net worth, which equals all total assets (like homes) minus all debts (like mortgages). Citing the Institute for Policy Studies, the article notes, "Between 1983 and 2013, the wealth of the median black household declined 75 percent (from $6,800 to $1,700), and the median Latino household declined 50 percent (from $4,000 to $2,000). At the same time, wealth for the median white household *increased* 14 percent from $102,000 to $116,800."

6. Rakesh Kochhar and Anthony Cilluffo, "How U.S. Wealth Inequality Has Changed since the Great Recession," Pew Research Center, November 1, 2017, http://www.pewresearch.org/fact-tank/2017/11/01/how-wealth -inequality-has-changed-in-the-u-s-since-the-great-recession-by-race -ethnicity-and-income/.

7. For example, see the Sentencing Project report sponsored by the United Nations: "Report of the Sentencing Project to the United Nations Human Rights Committee Regarding Racial Disparities in the U.S. Criminal Justice System," April 19, 2013, http://sentencingproject.org/publications/un-report-on-racial-disparities/.

8. Shankar Vedantam, Rhaina Cohen, Tara Boyle, and Camila Vargas-Restrepo, "Zipcode Destiny: The Persistent Power Of Place And Education," *Hidden Brain*, National Public Radio, November 12, 2018, https://www.npr.org/2018/11/12/666993130/zipcode-destiny-the-persistent-power-of-place-and-education.

9. Perceived ethnicity and race forcefully constrain a person's job opportunities. A well-publicized sociology experiment documented that job applicants who were presumed to be white (by their names) were more likely to get a job interview than were applicants who were presumed to be black (based on their names). This difference held, even when the résumés of white-sounding individuals showed that they were convicted felons. See Marianne Bertrand and Sendhil Mullainathan, "Are Emily and Greg More Employable than Lakisha and Jamal? A Field Experiment on Labor Market Discrimination," National Bureau of Economic Research Working Paper 9873 (July 2003), https://doi.org/10.3386/w9873.

10. For more on privilege, see Michael Eric Dyson, *Tears We Cannot Stop: A Sermon to White America* (New York: St. Martins, 2017). Dyson explains affirmative privilege as what one group does for its own members, specifically how the privilege of whites benefits other white people.

11. For another example of privileges in the criminal justice system granted based on race and wealth, see TED, "We Need to Talk about an Injustice: Bryan Stevenson," March 5, 2012, video, 23:41, https://www.youtube.com/watch?v=c2tOp7OxyQ8. As a defense lawyer, Stevenson once petitioned the judge to treat his teenage African American client charged with shoplifting with the same deference given to a European American corporate executive charged with tax fraud, as the judge considered his bail and release before trial.

Chapter 2

1. Luther E. Smith, in *Howard Thurman: Essential Writings*, ed. Luther E. Smith (Maryknoll, NY: Orbis, 2006), 89.

2. Attributed to Cornel West, professor of the practice of public philosophy at Harvard University.

3. Smith, in *Howard Thurman*, 89.

4. Presumably, because of limited space, the bishops do not mention various Asian American groups who also experienced severe oppression, such as during the internment of Japanese American citizens during World War II or the forced labor of Chinese Americans to build the transcontinental railroad in the nineteenth century.

5. See Audrey Smedley and Brian D. Smedley, "Race as Biology Is Fiction, Racism as a Social Problem Is Real: Anthropological and Historical Perspectives on the Social Construction of Race," *American Psychologist* 60, no. 1 (2005): 16, https://doi.org/10.1037/0003-066x.60.1.16.

6. See, for example, Erving Goffman, *Stigma: Notes on the Management of Spoiled Identity* (London: Penguin, 1990). Many other sociological studies have verified and extended Goffman's research in subsequent decades.

7. Robin DiAngelo, *White Fragility: Why It's So Hard for White People to Talk about Racism* (Boston: Beacon, 2018).

8. It seems that the only privilege we all accept uncritically is wealth, because of another national myth that hard work will yield success (as in "rags to riches"). See Richard Wilkinson, "How Economic Inequality Harms Societies," July 2011, TED video, 16:48, https://www.ted.com/talks/richard_wilkinson/.

9. For this discussion, see generally Dyson, *Tears We Cannot Stop*.

10. See generally Eviatar Zerubavel, *Taken for Granted: The Remarkable Power of the Unremarkable* (Princeton, NJ: Princeton University Press, 2018) and Eduardo Bonilla-Silva, *Racism without Racists*.

11. Peggy McIntosh, "White Privilege and Unpacking the Invisible Knapsack," in *Women: Images and Realities, A Multicultural Anthology*, ed. Suzanne Kelly, Gowri Parameswaran, and Nancy Schniedewind (New York: McGraw-Hill Education, 1995), 264–67.

12. Certainly, not all European immigrant groups have had equal power. Even among whites there has been a racialized hierarchy. See David R. Roediger, *Working Toward Whiteness: How America's Immigrants Became White: The Strange Journey from Ellis Island to the Suburbs* (New York: Basic, 2006).

13. Please see Questions for Study at the end of this chapter and resources at the end of the guide for recommendations to learn more about the history of various racial and ethnic groups in the United States.

14. While estimates vary, the population of Native Americans dropped from approximately 10 million in the sixteenth century to just over a

quarter million by 1900. See "Atrocities Against Native Americans," United to End Genocide, http://endgenocide.org/learn/past-genocides/native -americans/.

15. This does not mean to deny that between people of European descent there has not also been racial injustice and oppression, such as that against Irish or Italians. Sociologist David Roediger details the centuries of sort- ing and stacking of people along a spectrum, with whiteness as the most valued quality for social and political dominance. See Roediger, *Working Toward Whiteness*.

16. Bryan N. Massingale, *Racial Justice and the Catholic Church* (Mary- knoll, NY: Orbis, 2010), 47. See also Marilyn W. Nickels, "Thomas Wyatt Turner and the Federated Colored Catholics," *US Catholic Historian* 7, no. 2 (1988): 215–32.

17. Massingale, *Racial Justice*, 50.

18. John Paul II, Encyclical on the Social Concern of the Church (*Sol- licitudo Rei Socialis*), December 30, 1987, 39, emphasis original.

Chapter 3

1. The Roman Catholic Church bestows the title *Servant of God* upon people when the Vatican agrees to investigate their case for canonization.

2. Jeannine Hill Fletcher, *The Sin of White Supremacy: Christianity, Rac- ism, and Religious Diversity in America* (Maryknoll, NY: Orbis, 2017).

3. Laurie M. Cassidy and Alexander Mikulich, introduction to *Inter- rupting White Privilege: Catholic Theologians Break the Silence*, ed. Laurie M. Cassidy and Alexander Mikulich (Maryknoll, NY: Orbis, 2007), 5.

4. See Massingale, *Racial Justice*, 74–77, analyzing the US bishops' state- ments on race and racism prior to Open Wide Our Hearts.

5. Christopher Ingraham, "Three Quarters of Whites Don't Have Any Non-White Friends," *Washington Post*, August 25, 2014, https:// www.washingtonpost.com/news/wonk/wp/2014/08/25/three-quarters -of-whites-dont-have-any-non-white-friends/.

6. See the USCCB's resources about racism at "Combatting Racism— Parish Resources," http://www.usccb.org/issues-and-action/human-life -and-dignity/racism/parish-resources-on-racism.cfm. For a scholarly analy- sis of legal and social policies that perpetuate racism, see Daria Roithmayr, *Reproducing Racism: How Everyday Choices Lock in White Advantage* (New York: NYU Press, 2014).

7. Pope John Paul II, Encyclical Letter on the Hundredth Anniversary of *Rerum Novarum* (*Centesimus Annus*), May 1, 1991, http://w2.vatican.va /content/john-paul-ii/en/encyclicals/documents/hf_jp-ii_enc_01051991 _centesimus-annus.html.

8. For additional information, see Daniel K Finn, "Commentary on *Centesimus Annus* (On the Hundredth Anniversary of *Rerum Novarum*)," in Kenneth R. Himes, Lisa Sowle Cahill, Charles E. Curran, David Hollenbach, and Thomas A. Shannon, *Modern Catholic Social Teaching: Commentaries and Interpretations* (Washington, DC: Georgetown University Press, 2005), 436–66, 447.

9. Adapted from Roger Haight, "Prayer for Light and Courage," in Christian Iosso and Elizabeth L. Hinson-Hasty, *Prayers for the New Social Awakening: Inspired by the New Social Creed* (Louisville, KY: Westminster John Knox Press, 2008), 25–26. Used with permission.

Chapter 4

1. "See International Theological Commission, *Memory and Reconciliation*, no. 3.3, which quotes Augustine, *Sermon* 181, 5,7: 'The Church as a whole says: Forgive us our trespasses! Therefore, she has blemishes and wrinkles. But by means of confession the wrinkles are smoothed away and the blemishes washed clean. The Church stands in prayer in order to be purified by confession and, as long as men live on earth it will be so'" (n. 34).

2. Howard Thurman, in *Howard Thurman: Essential Writings*, ed. Luther E. Smith (Maryknoll, NY: Orbis, 2006), 142.

3. For more about the mandate to the Ad Hoc Committee, see "Ad Hoc Committee Against Racism—Mandate," http://www.usccb.org/issues-and -action/human-life-and-dignity/racism/ad-hoc-committee-against-racism -mandate.cfm.

4. "Combatting Racism—Parish Resources," http://www.usccb.org/issues -and-action/human-life-and-dignity/racism/parish-resources-on-racism .cfm. Parishes, Catholic organizations, and individual Catholics can begin here as they develop their own plans to combat racism and renovate our church culture.

5. More details about the community's journey to explore its past sins may be found at: "Our History of Slaveholding," Society of the Sacred Heart, https://rscj.org/history-slaveholding//. Information about the Georgetown University Working Group on Slavery and related efforts

of the University to explore its sale of enslaved people in the nineteenth century may be found at "The Georgetown Slavery Archive," https://slavery archive.georgetown.edu/.

6. These actions also respond to the bishops' command to all of us Catholics to educate ourselves about racism in our past (21). They give a few examples, such as visiting museums that honor and preserve the histories of African Americans or Native Americans. They mention saints whom we might use to spark reflection and discussions around historical and present injustices.

7. The resulting proceedings and podcasts are published at Brett Johnson Solomon, "Powering Toward Racial and Ethnic Justice in Our Common Home," Ignatian Center for Jesuit Education, Santa Clara University, https://www.scu.edu/ic/media--publications/explore-journal/spring-2018 -stories/powering-forward-toward-racial-and-ethnic-justice-in-our -common-home.html. The Jesuit School of Theology of Santa Clara University offers additional resources on racism at "Race Resources," Jesuit School of Theology, Santa Clara University, https://www.scu.edu/jst /resources/race-resources/. I am familiar with these initiatives because I serve on that faculty. However, many other Catholic colleges and universities offer excellent resources to begin discussing race issues in the United States, past or present. Georgetown University's multiyear effort to acknowledge responsibility for the 272 enslaved people it sold 200 years ago to raise cash, and to offer reparations to their descendants, is a noteworthy example.

8. Consider Bryan Stevenson, *Just Mercy: A Story of Justice and Redemption* (New York: Spiegel & Grau, 2015), which describes the tragedy of the US criminal justice system with burdens unfairly imposed upon black and brown defendants. Through data and stories of individuals caught in the system, Stevenson shows how this system is skewed to suspect, scrutinize, interrogate, distrust, and over-punish people of color and immigrants.

9. We recall learning in chapter 1 that there are no genetic markers for the conventional racial labels. Therefore, when the bishops refer to crossing racial boundaries, they mean the cultural delineation most frequently used. Crossing racial boundaries will help us grasp both the impact of unjust racially motivated stereotypes as well as the meaninglessness of the demarcations.

10. Ingraham, "Three Quarters of Whites."

11. See John Eligon, "The 'Some of My Best Friends Are Black' Defense," *New York Times*, February 16, 2019, https://www.nytimes.com/2019/02/16 /sunday-review/ralph-northam-blackface-friends.html, which describes how white people can remain ignorant of their own racist biases and stereotypes despite experiences of living, learning, and socializing with people of different races.

12. Jean Vanier, *Community and Growth: Our Pilgrimage Together* (New York: Paulist, 1989), 6.

13. Massingale, *Racial Justice*, 87.

14. Massingale summarizes here the work of ethicist Erik K. Yamamoto in *Interracial Justice: Conflict and Reconciliation in Post-Civil Rights America* (New York: New York University Press, 1999), 97–102.

15. Although this prayer is often attributed to St. Oscar Romero, archbishop of San Salvador, it was written by Bishop Ken Untener for Cardinal Dearden on the occasion of the Mass for Deceased Priests, October 25, 1979. See "Prophets of a Future Not Our Own," USCCB, http://www.usccb.org/prayer-and-worship/prayers-and-devotions/prayers /prophets-of-a-future-not-our-own.cfm.

Conclusion

1. Adapted version of Litany for Racial Justice by Wehn-In Ng, from *That All May Be One*—A Resource for Educating toward Racial Justice (The United Church of Canada, 2004), pp. 77–78. Reprinted with permission.

For Further Reading

Introduction
For an accessible overview of Catholic social thought, including its nine key themes and recent papal teachings, see:

Massaro, Thomas. *Living Justice: Catholic Social Teaching in Action*. 3rd ed. Lanham, MD: Rowman & Littlefield, 2015.

For a good general overview of racial injustice as a cultural problem and as a social sin, consider:

Massingale, Bryan. *Racial Justice and the Catholic Church*. Maryknoll: Orbis, 2010.
Other references below update the topic since 2010.

Chapter 1
There are many books that offer a sociological explanation of racism as a structural injustice in United States culture. Here is a selection:

Bonilla-Silva, Eduardo. *Racism without Racists: Color-Blind Racism and the Persistence of Racial Inequality in America*. 4th ed. Lanham, MD: Rowman & Littlefield, 2014.
Delgado, Richard, and Jean Stefancic. *Critical Race Theory: An Introduction*. Vol. 20. New York: NYU Press, 2017.
DiAngelo, Robin. *White Fragility: Why It's so Hard for White People to Talk about Racism*. Boston: Beacon Press, 2018.
Kendi, Ibram X. *Stamped from the Beginning: The Definitive History of Racist Ideas in America*. New York: Random House, 2017.

Smedley, Audrey. *Race in North America: Origin and Evolution of a Worldview*. London: Routledge, 2018.

Chapter 2

For a comprehensive overview of racism as it emerged and took hold in US history, read:

Roediger, David R. *How Race Survived US History: From Settlement and Slavery to the Obama Phenomenon*. Brooklyn, NY: Verso, 2008.

Because the experiences and identities of the various racial and ethnic groups in the United States are so varied, the following books may be of interest as reliable studies for various population segments in the United States:

African American experience:

Alexander, Michelle. *The New Jim Crow: Mass Incarceration in the Age of Colorblindness*. New York: New Press, 2012.

Asian American experience:

Lee, Erika. *The Making of Asian America: A History*. New York: Simon & Schuster, 2015.

European American experience:

Painter, Nell Irvin. *The History of White People*. New York: W. W. Norton, 2010.

Latinx experience:

Gonzalez, Juan. *Harvest of Empire: A History of Latinos in America*. London: Penguin, 2001.

Native American experience:

Dunbar-Ortiz, Roxanne. *An Indigenous Peoples' History of the United States*. Vol. 3. Boston: Beacon, 2014.

To discover the ideologies, laws, and policies that shaped and secured privileges for whites throughout US history, read:

Goza, Joel Edward. *America's Unholy Ghosts: The Racist Roots of Our Faith and Politics*. Eugene, OR: Wipf & Stock, 2019.

Klarman, Michael J. *Unfinished Business: Racial Equality in American History*. New York: Oxford University Press, 2007.

Roediger, David R. *The Wages of Whiteness: Race and the Making of the American Working Class*. Brooklyn, NY: Verso, 1999.

Roithmayr, Daria. *Reproducing Racism: How Everyday Choices Lock In White Advantage*. New York: NYU Press, 2014.

Rothstein, Richard. *The Color of Law: A Forgotten History of How Our Government Segregated America*. New York: Liveright, 2017.

Chapter 3

For theological discussions of racism, social sin, and racial injustice, see:

Copeland, M. Shawn. *Enfleshing Freedom: Body, Race, and Being*. Minneapolis: Fortress, 2010.

Davis, Cyprian, and Jamie Therese Phelps, eds. *Stamped with the Image of God: African Americans as God's Image in Black*. Maryknoll, NY: Orbis, 2003.

Fletcher, Jeannine Hill. *The Sin of White Supremacy: Christianity, Racism, and Religious Diversity in America*. Maryknoll, NY: Orbis, 2017.

Grimes, Katie Walker. *Christ Divided: Antiblackness as Corporate Vice*. Minneapolis: Fortress, 2017.

Lloyd, Vincent W., and Andrew Prevot, eds. *Anti-blackness and Christian Ethics*. Maryknoll, NY: Orbis, 2017.

Massingale, Bryan N. "Has the Silence Been Broken? Catholic Theological Ethics and Racial Justice." *Theological Studies* 75, no. 1 (2014): 133–55.

Wallis, Jim. *America's Original Sin: Racism, White Privilege, and the Bridge to a New America*. Grand Rapids, MI: Brazos , 2016.

Chapter 4

There are many accessible books that narrate the US experience of racism, individual and structural. This list contains only a few suggestions:

Coates, Ta-Nehisi. *Between the World and Me*. New York: Spiel & Grau, 2015.

Dyson, Michael Eric. *Tears We Cannot Stop: A Sermon to White America*. New York: St. Martin's, 2017.

Glaude, Eddie S., Jr. *Democracy in Black: How Race Still Enslaves the American Soul*. New York: Broadway, 2017.

Hart, Drew G. I. *Trouble I've Seen: Changing the Way the Church Views Racism*. Harrisonburg, VA: Herald, 2016.

To explore actions taken by Christian churches to resist racism, consider:

Barndt, Joseph. *Becoming an Anti-Racist Church: Journeying toward Wholeness*. Minneapolis: Fortress, 2011.

Harvey, Jennifer. *Dear White Christians: For Those Still Longing for Racial Reconciliation*. Grand Rapids, MI: William B. Eerdmans, 2014.

Rice, Lincoln. *Healing the Racial Divide: A Catholic Racial Justice Framework Inspired by Dr. Arthur Falls*. Eugene, OR: Wipf & Stock, 2014.

Wilson-Hartgrove, Jonathan. *Reconstructing the Gospel: Finding Freedom from Slaveholder Religion*. Downers Grove, IL: InterVarsity, 2018.

There are also many fine resources to begin anti-racism actions, in addition to those offered by the United States Conference of Catholic Bishops. Many are available online by searching terms such as "anti-racist activism," "racial healing," "white allies," "restorative justice," "reparations," and similar terms. Many Christian denominations offer extensive materials freely available on their website, which can guide a parish or school's anti-racist work.